CROSSWORDS

Published in 2022 by Welbeck
An imprint of Welbeck Non-Fiction Limited
part of Welbeck Publishing Group
Offices in: London – 20 Mortimer Street, London W1T 3JW
& Sydney – 205 Commonwealth Street, Surry Hills 2010
www.welbeckpublishing.com

Editorial: Tall Tree Limited
Design: Tall Tree Limited and Eliana Holder

A CIP catalogue for this book is available from the British Library.

ISBN: 978-1-80279-668-1

Printed in the United Kingdom

10 9 8 7 6 5 4 3 2 1

CROSSWORDS

More than 100 puzzles to test your word power and general knowledge

Dr Gareth Moore

WELBECK

INTRODUCTION

Welcome to this wonderful crossword collection, packed from cover to cover with 120 puzzles, including 20 smaller crosswords and 100 premium-size 15x15 puzzles.

To solve each puzzle, just work out the answer to each across and down clue and write the answers into the grid in the appropriate directions, starting from the corresponding clue numbers, with one letter per square.

Numbers in parentheses after each clue reveal the number of letters in each answer, matching the number of spaces in the grid. Multiple numbers separated with a comma indicate multiple words; numbers separated with a hyphen indicate hyphenated words. Best of luck with the puzzles!

Dr Gareth Moore, London

SOLUTION SEE PAGE 226

1	2		3		4		5		6	
■		■		■		■		■		■
7						■	8			
■		■	■	■		■		■	■	■
9			10		■	11			12	
■		■		■	■	■		■		■
13					■	14				
■	■	■		■	15	■	■	■		■
16	17			■	18		19			
■		■		■		■		■		■
20										

ACROSS

1. Doubt (11)
7. Fairly (6)
8. Yoga expert (4)
9. Orbit (5)
11. Tells you the time (5)
13. Charred remains (5)
14. Behaved (5)
16. Common soft drink (4)
18. The sale of goods (6)
20. Round brackets (11)

DOWN

2. Beginners (7)
3. Geologist's time measure (3)
4. Playthings (4)
5. Extremely happy (7)
6. Item of clothing, informally (3)
10. Get ready (7)
12. Fissure (7)
15. Young troublemaker (4)
17. Egg cells (3)
19. Foot extremity (3)

SOLUTION SEE PAGE 226

ACROSS

1. Efficiencies (9)
7. Splits (5)
8. Common birch-family tree (5)
10. Stiffly formal (4)
11. Religious festival (6)
14. Translated for the deaf, perhaps (6)
15. Soot particle (4)
17. Grub (5)
19. Greeting (5)
20. Set up (9)

DOWN

2. Guile (7)
3. Central facial feature (4)
4. Nasty person, informally (6)
5. Objective (3)
6. Offer of marriage (8)
9. Response to a stimulus (8)
12. Akin (7)
13. Stead (6)
16. Lout (4)
18. Seventeenth Greek letter (3)

SOLUTION SEE PAGE 227

1	2		3		4		5		6	
■		■		■		■		■		■
7										
■		■		■	■	■		■		■
8		9		10		11		12		
■	■		■		■		■		■	■
13	14		15				16		17	
■		■		■	■	■		■		■
18					19					
■		■		■		■		■		■
20										

ACROSS

1. Dismantle (11)
7. Upsetting (11)
8. Cardiac arrest (5,6)
13. Powered cutting blade (8,3)
18. However (11)
20. Visual lacks of balance (11)

DOWN

2. Upper classes (5)
3. Exterior (5)
4. Prosecute (3)
5. Start again (5)
6. Sceptic (5)
9. It's mostly oxygen and nitrogen (3)
10. Nineteenth Greek letter (3)
11. Hot or iced drink (3)
12. TV breaks (3)
14. Computer app identifiers (5)
15. Fatty part of milk (5)
16. Chief (5)
17. Flight seat choice (5)
19. Gardening tool (3)

SOLUTION SEE PAGE 227

1	2		3		4			5		6
■		■		■		■	■		■	
7				■	8					
■		■		■		■	■		■	
9					■	10	11		12	
■		■		■	■	■		■		■
13		14			■	15				
	■		■	■	16	■		■		■
17						■	18			
	■		■	■		■		■		■
19										

ACROSS

1. Changed; modified (11)
7. Float through the air (4)
8. Interrupt (4,2)
9. Social trip, perhaps (5)
10. All possible (5)
13. Find the mass of (5)
15. Declare (5)
17. Theatrical smoke (3,3)
18. Postal delivery (4)
19. Readiness to provide assistance (11)

DOWN

2. Come to understand (7)
3. Zero (7)
4. Small lies (4)
5. Dull paint finish (5)
6. Gloomy and drab (5)
11. Required dietary nutrient (7)
12. Keeps (7)
13. Breadth (5)
14. Short, pastoral poem (5)
16. List of choices (4)

5

SOLUTION SEE PAGE 228

ACROSS

1. Making self-running (10)
7. Worldwide (6)
8. Cries uncontrollably (4)
9. Stays in a tent (5)
11. Discovers (5)
13. Plant barb (5)
14. Horse's whinny (5)
16. Shells, eg (4)
18. Automatons (6)
20. Confessedly (10)

DOWN

2. Let loose (7)
3. Part of a monarch's regalia (3)
4. Troubles; afflicts (4)
5. Fill with spirit (7)
6. Small lump (3)
10. Execute (7)
12. Made up of 0s and 1s (7)
15. 'Curses!' (4)
17. Emu's extinct relative (3)
19. A free win, in sport (3)

SOLUTION SEE PAGE 228

ACROSS

3. Humorous (5)
6. Briskly, in music (3,4)
7. Large stream (5)
8. Heavy clubs (5)
9. It's not a solid or liquid (3)
11. Beneath (5)
13. Dog rope (5)
15. Despicable person, informally (3)
18. Given up (5)
19. Blood-pumping organ (5)
20. Improve (7)
21. Connected with cables (5)

DOWN

1. Revolve (6)
2. Hadrian or Augustus (7)
3. Not casual (6)
4. Main body of a basilica (4)
5. Long ago times, in literature (4)
10. A few more than a few (7)
12. Intoxicated (slang) (6)
14. Oration (6)
16. Masticate (4)
17. Impartial (4)

7

SOLUTION SEE PAGE 229

ACROSS

1. Female artisan (11)
7. Handle incorrectly (6)
8. Unchanged (4)
9. Before all the others (5)
11. Really fast (5)
13. Luminous (5)
14. Stylistic category (5)
16. Rotisserie rod (4)
18. Secured with a key (6)
20. Fairly accurate (11)

DOWN

2. Elevating (7)
3. Respiratory disease (3)
4. Notices (4)
5. Barely known (7)
6. Division, as in a company (3)
10. Briefer (7)
12. Rectify (7)
15. Bend a limb (4)
17. Brief clock chime (3)
19. Online video device (3)

SOLUTION SEE PAGE 229

1	2		3		4			5		6
■		■		■		■	■		■	
7						■	8			
■		■		■		■	■		■	
9				■	10		11		12	
■		■		■	■	■		■		■
13		14			15	■	16			
	■		■	■		■		■		■
17				■	18					
	■		■	■		■		■		■
19										

ACROSS

1. Kill someone important (11)
7. Better weather (6)
8. Metal rods (4)
9. Lower-arm bone (4)
10. Bathed, perhaps (6)
13. Resides (6)
16. 'My bad!' (4)
17. Objections (4)
18. Working as a thespian (6)
19. Head of an order of chivalry (5,6)

DOWN

2. Drink some liquid (7)
3. Type of international post (7)
4. Twist (5)
5. Disconcert (5)
6. Abated (5)
11. Flattens out (7)
12. Cost (7)
13. Fix a computer program (5)
14. Additional (5)
15. Oiliness (5)

9

SOLUTION SEE PAGE 230

ACROSS

1. Made a formal decision on a matter (11)
6. Gunfire for bringing down aircraft (3-3)
7. Sullen (4)
8. Lies in wait (5)
11. Rot (5)
12. More peculiar (5)
13. Very pale, as with fright (5)
17. Network of crossing lines (4)
18. Grain container (6)
19. Bullion deposits in a central bank (4,7)

DOWN

1. Take advantage of (5)
2. Special playing card (5)
3. Irritates; annoys (4)
4. Property location (7)
5. Imitate (7)
9. Be put through (7)
10. Worked dough (7)
14. Extremely energetic (5)
15. Audacity (5)
16. Butter used in Indian cooking (4)

10

SOLUTION SEE PAGE 230

ACROSS

1. Weak; feeble (9)
8. Incident (5)
9. First-rate (5)
10. Glowing fire remnants (6)
12. Metallic element found in brass (4)
14. Clothed (4)
15. Unneeded extras (6)
17. Instrument with black and white keys (5)
18. Japanese bamboo-sword fencing (5)
20. Ingredient (9)

DOWN

2. Maiden name indicator (3)
3. With no part left out (6)
4. Fewer in number (4)
5. More cheery (7)
6. Magnifying device (9)
7. Food blender (9)
11. Bluster (7)
13. Verbal (6)
16. Cleaning substance (4)
19. Convent dweller (3)

11

SOLUTION SEE PAGE 231

ACROSS

3. Traverse (5)
6. Enchanting (7)
7. Funeral poem (5)
8. Claw (5)
9. Jewel (3)
11. Enjoyed (5)
13. Make a comeback (5)
15. Wild animal's home (3)
18. Vinegar and lemon juice, eg (5)
19. Japanese poem (5)
20. Suffered distress (7)
21. Kicks (5)

DOWN

1. Italian sausage variety (6)
2. Strongly prejudiced (7)
3. Intelligent (6)
4. Walkie-talkie sign-off (4)
5. States (4)
10. Agreed (7)
12. Fixes computer software (6)
14. Women (6)
16. Hit hard (4)
17. Pottery furnace (4)

SOLUTION SEE PAGE 231

	1	2		3		4		5		

ACROSS

1. Products (9)
7. Sends a parcel (5)
8. Black-and-white horse? (5)
10. Journey (4)
11. Unhurriedly (6)
14. Infested (6)
15. Engage a gearwheel (4)
17. About (5)
19. Radioactive gas (5)
20. Lawyers (9)

DOWN

2. Consolidated (7)
3. Sample (4)
4. Sudoku, maybe (6)
5. Tidal retreat (3)
6. Understood only by those with specialist knowledge (8)
9. 'Take your pick' (8)
12. Monday or Tuesday, eg (7)
13. Smoothly, in music (6)
16. Husk remains (4)
18. Long, deep track (3)

13

SOLUTION SEE PAGE 232

ACROSS

1. Devoting (10)
6. Oleaginous (6)
7. Small mark (4)
10. Topic (7)
12. A person's home, informally (3)
13. Fantasy menace (3)
14. Official trade ban (7)
15. Green, carpeting plant that grows in damp habitats (4)
18. Gets rid of (6)
19. Radio show presenter (4,6)

DOWN

1. Dirt-ridden whirlwind (4,5)
2. Disadvantages (9)
3. Take part in the hope of winning (7)
4. Opposite of outs (3)
5. Baby's first word? (3)
8. Book with a flexible cover (9)
9. Laboriously (9)
11. Smoker's vice (7)
16. Unusual (3)
17. Certain sibling (3)

14

SOLUTION SEE PAGE 232

ACROSS

1. Nomenclature (11)
7. Unwanted email (4)
8. Unmoving (6)
9. Swift curving movement (5)
10. Leaf pore (5)
13. Vulgar (5)
15. Nice weather, perhaps (5)
17. Secret (6)
18. Frozen rain (4)
19. Encircling (11)

DOWN

2. Authorize (7)
3. People in a group (7)
4. A bird's home (4)
5. Exceed (5)
6. Agave with sharp leaves (5)
11. Came into contact with (7)
12. Bring up (7)
13. Lawn (5)
14. Happen (5)
16. Fashionable young man (4)

15

SOLUTION SEE PAGE 233

1	2		3		4		5		6	

7							8			

9			10			11			12	

13						14				

15

16	17				18		19			

20										

ACROSS

1. Specifying (11)
7. Ensnarl (6)
8. Crudely offensive (4)
9. Huts (5)
11. Stores (5)
13. Lopsided (5)
14. Ornamental quartz (5)
16. Slams against (4)
18. Source (6)
20. Heated debate (11)

DOWN

2. Instructs (7)
3. Fix at a particular level (3)
4. Made things up (4)
5. Particularly revealing (7)
6. Fresh (3)
10. Recessed (4-3)
12. Ingresses (7)
15. Not in stereo or surround? (4)
17. Back in time (3)
19. Frozen water (3)

16

SOLUTION SEE PAGE 233

1	2		3		4			5		6
7							8			
9					10		11		12	
13		14			15		16			
17					18					
19										

ACROSS

1. Neck of a stringed instrument (11)
7. Confusion (6)
8. Cross-border document (4)
9. Action word (4)
10. Paved road (6)
13. Very serious (6)
16. Rear of the human body (4)
17. Birds hunted for food (4)
18. Collect (6)
19. Belief in nothing beyond what is material (11)

DOWN

2. Before birth (2,5)
3. Complaint (7)
4. Charges per periods (5)
5. Not yet dead (5)
6. Outline drawing (5)
11. Like an automaton (7)
12. Surpasses (7)
13. Eighteenth Greek letter (5)
14. Feeble or pathetic thing, informally (5)
15. Time without sun (5)

17

SOLUTION SEE PAGE 234

ACROSS

3. Quality beef cut (5)
6. Deliberate (7)
7. Fault (5)
8. Less (5)
9. Tailless, large primate (3)
11. Ascends (5)
13. Fasten (5)
15. Payable (3)
18. Steered a car (5)
19. In front (5)
20. Mends (7)
21. Vacant (5)

DOWN

1. Toasted Italian sandwiches (6)
2. Decreased (7)
3. Rests (6)
4. Merit (4)
5. Adjust type spacing (4)
10. Everlasting (7)
12. Various (6)
14. Goes over the top of (6)
16. Strong wind (4)
17. Low in pitch (4)

18

SOLUTION SEE PAGE 234

1		2		3		4		5		6
	■		■		■		■		■	
7							■	8		
	■	■	■		■		■		■	
9		10		■	11					
	■		■	12	■		■		■	
13						■	14			
	■		■		■	15	■	■	■	
16			■	17				18		
	■		■		■		■		■	
19										

ACROSS

1. Restorative; healing (11)
7. Try (7)
8. Fast jog (3)
9. Drinks slowly (4)
11. Not susceptible (6)
13. By mouth (6)
14. Following straight after (4)
16. Tit for _ (3)
17. Ape (7)
19. Prove (11)

DOWN

1. Moved (11)
2. Chew and swallow (3)
3. Charity for the poor (4)
4. Lay to rest within something (6)
5. Torment (7)
6. Focus (11)
10. Ghost (7)
12. Catchphrase (6)
15. Worry (4)
18. Grazing land (3)

19

SOLUTION SEE PAGE 235

ACROSS

1. Not wanted (9)
8. Lowest point (5)
9. Foundation (5)
10. Specialist (6)
12. Walk through water (4)
14. Remainder (4)
15. Excellent (6)
17. Sweet, juicy stone fruit (5)
18. Writing (5)
20. Noticing (9)

DOWN

2. Get the _, to be selected (3)
3. Software bugs (6)
4. Taxis (4)
5. Slip-up (7)
6. Butt in (9)
7. Joined together (9)
11. Corridor (7)
13. Resulting product (6)
16. Foot covering (4)
19. Confess to something: _ up (3)

SOLUTION SEE PAGE 235

ACROSS

1. Regarding feelings (11)
6. Not uniform (6)
7. Animal doctors (4)
8. Cowboy's rope (5)
11. Gather (5)
12. Prophet (5)
13. Fresher (5)
17. Attempt (4)
18. State of repair (6)
19. Sped up (11)

DOWN

1. Of the same value (5)
2. Conforms (5)
3. Pig grunt (4)
4. Hostile (7)
5. Green, leafy salad vegetable (7)
9. Relating to water (7)
10. Short facial hairs (7)
14. Take forcefully (5)
15. Speedy (5)
16. Ancient writing symbol (4)

SOLUTION SEE PAGE 236

ACROSS

6. Exasperate (7)
7. Inner self (5)
9. Slip (4)
10. Unrhymed poem (5,5)
11. Attractive; alluring (8)
13. 'Finally!' (2,4)
15. Trip over (4)
17. By surprise, as in 'taken _' (5)
18. Learned (4)
19. Vigorous (6)
20. Angry driving (4,4)
23. Gratefully (10)
26. Crazes (4)
27. Like a blast from the past (5)
28. Normally (7)

DOWN

1. Of top-class cookery (6,4)
2. Battle (6)
3. Soft, white cheese (4)
4. Rucksack (8)
5. Advisor (4)
6. First-class, informally (5)
8. Helps (7)
12. Seat (5)
14. Avoiding publicity (3,7)
16. One more (7)
17. Natural disaster (3,2,3)
21. Political sanctuary (6)
22. Pious (5)
24. Musical tone (4)
25. Gaudy (4)

22

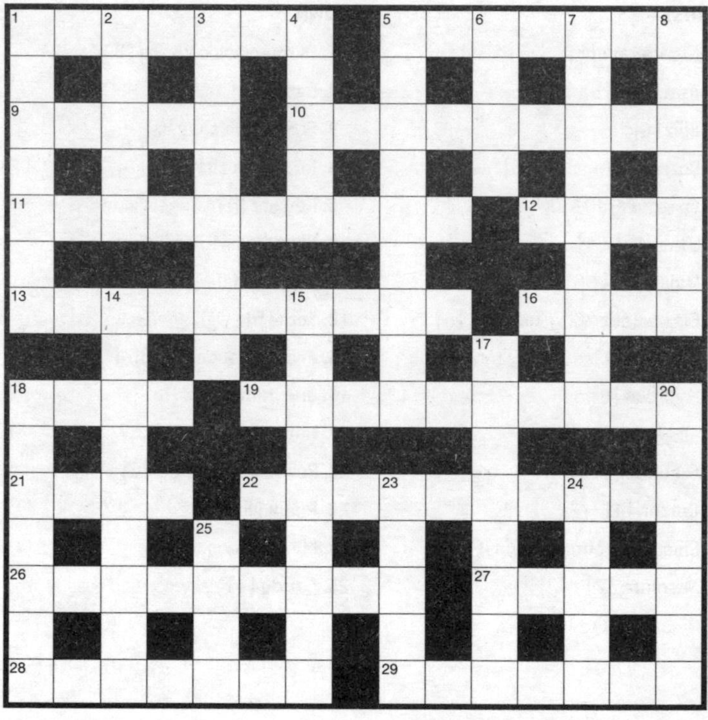

SOLUTION SEE PAGE 236

ACROSS

1. Groom's number two (4,3)

5. As a single group (2,5)

9. Ill-suited (5)

10. Spying (9)

11. Vanishes (10)

12. Clue (4)

13. Mail store (4,6)

16. Excitement (4)

18. Female domestic servant (4)

19. Not harmful to the environment (10)

21. Glided (4)

22. Defeating (10)

26. Remarkably (9)

27. Speak without a script (2-3)

28. Absolute quiet (7)

29. Give a right to (7)

DOWN

1. To strengthen physically (5,2)

2. Lathers (5)

3. Figure of speech (8)

4. Nephew's sister (5)

5. Derived from observation (9)

6. Satellite (4)

7. Piece of data (9)

8. Someone eligible to vote (7)

14. Religious (9)

15. Apparent worth (4,5)

17. Unlettered (8)

18. Buildings for antiquities (7)

20. Readable (7)

23. Correspond in sound endings (5)

24. Small, water-surrounded area of land (5)

25. Unstable subatomic particle (4)

23

SOLUTION SEE PAGE 237

ACROSS

7. Flaming (5)

8. Morose (4)

9. Thick Japanese pasta strips (4)

11. Get back (6)

12. Julian or Gregorian, eg (8)

13. Twelfth Night visitors (4)

15. Letter before theta (3)

16. Official order (5)

19. Assembly (7)

20. File-system groups (7)

23. Sun-dried brick (5)

25. Obtained (3)

26. Jetty (4)

28. Obliterate (8)

30. Releases (6)

32. Unit of distance (4)

33. Waiter's carrier (4)

34. Horse (5)

DOWN

1. Morsel (4)

2. Invention (8)

3. Bitterly cold (7)

4. Stroll (5)

5. Destroyed (6)

6. Bright star (4)

10. Receive from your parents (7)

14. Avert (5)

17. Profane expression (5)

18. Nasal opening (7)

21. Sets down (8)

22. Intellectual (7)

24. Wanting a baby, informally (6)

27. Thin fogs (5)

29. Periods of time (4)

31. Level; not at an angle (4)

24

SOLUTION SEE PAGE 237

ACROSS

9. Attain (7)
10. Sovereign's stand-in (7)
11. Left office (7)
12. Mundane (7)
13. Arrive and depart as you please (4,3,2)
15. Fuming (5)
16. Withdraw from confrontation (4,3)
19. Long-distance clubs (7)
20. Horned African animal (5)
21. Exchanged (9)
25. Sends in a form, perhaps (7)
26. Large, lavish meal (7)
28. Portable lamp (7)
29. Outline drawings (7)

DOWN

1. Cloth (6)
2. Beat (6)
3. Be dressed in (4)
4. Obligatory (6)
5. Give excessive work (8)
6. Examine minutely (10)
7. Annoy (8)
8. Lays out text (8)
14. Said sorry (10)
16. Rock crustacean (8)
17. Newspaper snippet (8)
18. Adjusting a camera lens (8)
22. Not a single person (6)
23. However (6)
24. Abhor (6)
27. Depose (4)

25

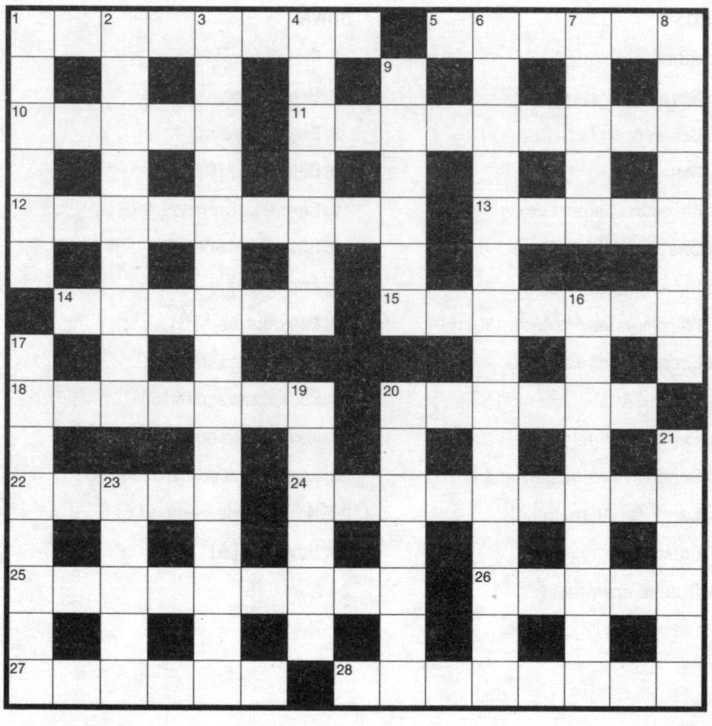

SOLUTION SEE PAGE 238

ACROSS

1. Ripe for picking (2,6)

5. Burn (6)

10. Ornamental headgear (5)

11. Utterly (9)

12. Citrus fruit preserve (9)

13. Unaffiliated record label (5)

14. Immensely (6)

15. Flabbergasted (7)

18. Become brighter (5,2)

20. Loll (6)

22. Express contempt, perhaps (5)

24. Digging machine (9)

25. Surgical procedure (9)

26. Squads (5)

27. Breaks into parts (6)

28. Clergyman (8)

DOWN

1. Eventually (2,4)

2. Flight of steps (9)

3. Actually (2,1,6,2,4)

4. Wife (slang) (3,4)

6. Career summary (10,5)

7. Inflexible (5)

8. Impetuous people (8)

9. Possessors (6)

16. Very unpleasant experience (9)

17. Paper-cutting tool (8)

19. Add to the start (6)

20. Grant permission (7)

21. Rubbed out (6)

23. Exactly right (5)

26

SOLUTION SEE PAGE 238

ACROSS

6. Quantities (7)

7. Offensiveness (5)

9. Window ledge (4)

10. Putting together (10)

11. Two-wheeled vehicles (8)

13. Compensation (6)

15. A mark from a wound (4)

17. Make a speech (5)

18. High (4)

19. Age (4,2)

20. Centuries (8)

23. Printed media in general (10)

26. Privy to, as in a secret (2,2)

27. Raise a glass to (5)

28. Meal-preparation room (7)

DOWN

1. Disparate group of dubious people (6,4)

2. Imply (6)

3. Questions (4)

4. Trade (8)

5. Bird's beak (4)

6. Corroboration (5)

8. Mixed-breed dog (7)

12. Shatter (5)

14. Indisputable (10)

16. Set of athletic exercises (7)

17. Contrary (8)

21. Nullify (6)

22. Submerge (5)

24. Fertile soil of clay and sand (4)

25. Signs a contract (4)

27

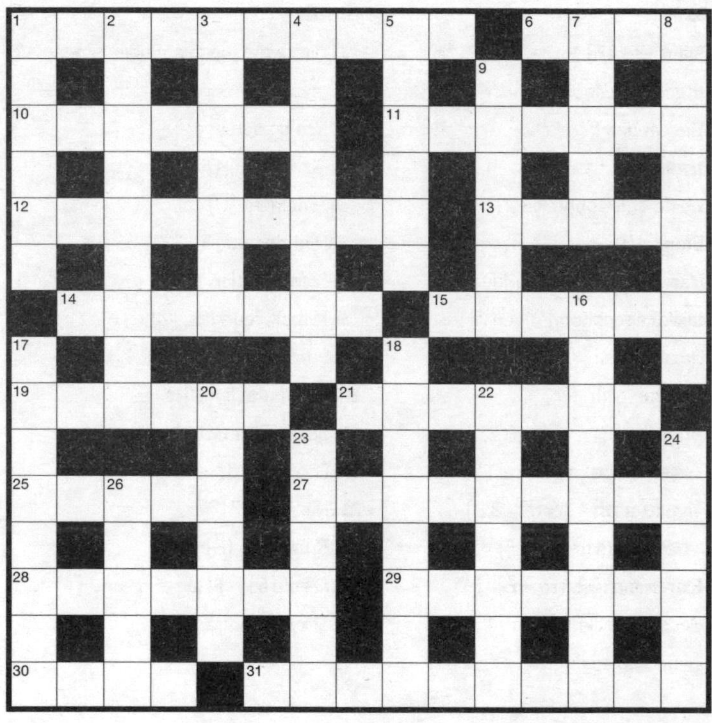

SOLUTION SEE PAGE 239

ACROSS

1. Denotes (10)
6. Stylish and fashionable (4)
10. Descended from a common maternal ancestor (7)
11. White pool sphere (3,4)
12. Bought (9)
13. Marshy lake or river outlet (5)
14. Surface rock formation (7)
15. Organ rupture (6)
19. At some point (3,3)
21. Modesty (7)
25. Entire spectrum (5)
27. Acquittal (9)
28. Electromotive force (7)
29. Extremely insulting (7)
30. Decorative cloth band (4)
31. Again and again (10)

DOWN

1. From the top, in music (2,4)
2. Tea sweetener (5,4)
3. On-screen image (7)
4. Antipathy (8)
5. Encipher (6)
7. Ponderous (5)
8. Ethnic (8)
9. Small, rounded stone (6)
16. 'It doesn't matter' (5,4)
17. Pardons (8)
18. Convince (8)
20. Relating to the stars (6)
22. Fatigue (7)
23. Stay attached (6)
24. Just (6)
26. Men (5)

SOLUTION SEE PAGE 239

ACROSS

7. Jazz variant (5)
8. Do injury to, as in pride (4)
9. Thick string (4)
11. Least wild (6)
12. Dependable (8)
13. Eye up (4)
15. Guys (3)
16. Antitoxin (5)
19. Overseas officials (7)
20. Carnivorous South American fish (7)
23. Large animal (5)
25. Deuce (3)
26. Young salmon (4)
28. Not functional at all (8)
30. Surrounded (6)
32. Extruded square, perhaps (4)
33. Broad valley (4)
34. Reddish-brown (5)

DOWN

1. Second Greek letter (4)
2. Despairing (8)
3. Splitting apart (7)
4. Coral island (5)
5. Make (6)
6. Gemstone (4)
10. Falter (7)
14. Large, white waterbird (5)
17. Court official (5)
18. Intolerance (7)
21. Added on (8)
22. Completely (7)
24. Nun (6)
27. Bear (5)
29. Object word (4)
31. Send forth (4)

SOLUTION SEE PAGE 240

ACROSS

9. Parent's father (7)

10. Tremulous bird chirp (7)

11. Ocular cleansing lotion (7)

12. Floating mass of frozen water (7)

13. Common type of pasta (9)

15. Accounts inspection (5)

16. Gives a new title to (7)

19. Fail as a business (2,5)

20. Glossy fabric (5)

21. Uncared-for (9)

25. Critiques in the media (7)

26. Boils so as to thicken (7)

28. Profound (7)

29. Trellis (7)

DOWN

1. Is of the same opinion (6)

2. SLR, eg (6)

3. Gist (4)

4. Small, sealed bag (6)

5. Hitting (8)

6. Classic writings (10)

7. Was present at (8)

8. Less dark (8)

14. Member of "homo sapiens" (5,5)

16. Hold back (8)

17. Birth occasion (8)

18. Forbidding (8)

22. Distort (6)

23. Ploy (6)

24. Made haste (6)

27. Small round marks or spots (4)

SOLUTION SEE PAGE 240

ACROSS

1. Drab (6)
4. Multitudes (6)
9. Employs (4)
10. Food blenders (10)
11. Taken without permission (6)
12. Broadcast (8)
13. Governed by bishops (9)
15. Places to sleep (4)
16. Pond organism (4)
17. Variety (9)
21. Accepting (8)
22. Housing (6)
24. Inexplicable (10)
25. Send a package by post (4)
26. Firstborn (6)
27. Allot (6)

DOWN

1. Non-portable computer (7)
2. Artist's stand (5)
3. Verbally attack (3,4)
5. They might be soap or comic (6)
6. Calamities (9)
7. Twists ligaments or muscles (7)
8. Paradox (13)
14. Proposed (9)
16. Painkiller (7)
18. Forgives (7)
19. Stress (7)
20. Large, tusked marine mammal (6)
23. Japanese cuisine (5)

SOLUTION SEE PAGE 241

ACROSS

6. Visitor (7)
7. Relating to charged particles (5)
9. Adroit (4)
10. Watched over (10)
11. Underground burial gallery (8)
13. Soldiers (6)
15. Disclose secret information (4)
17. Asked, as a question (5)
18. Dweeb (4)
19. Concern (6)
20. Gives advice (8)
23. Maximum velocity (5,5)
26. Something to scratch? (4)
27. Follow as a result (5)
28. Diary (7)

DOWN

1. Removable book cover (4,6)
2. Complete disaster (6)
3. Pace (4)
4. Moved from one region to another (8)
5. Opposed to (4)
6. Letter after eta (5)
8. Less expensive (7)
12. Fundamental (5)
14. All-knowing (10)
16. Specimen (7)
17. Side by side (8)
21. False (6)
22. Nearby (5)
24. In the past (archaic) (4)
25. Personal magnetism (slang) (4)

32

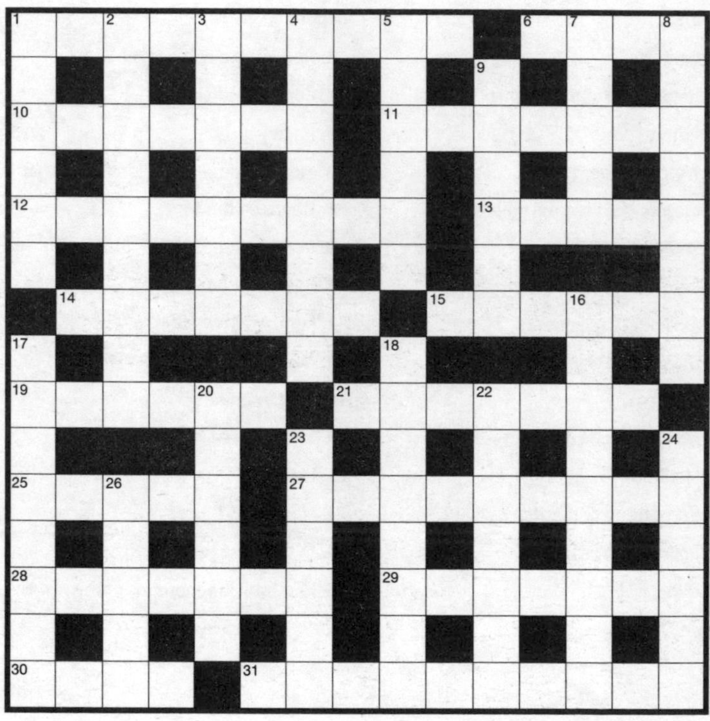

SOLUTION SEE PAGE 241

ACROSS

1. Innately (10)
6. Way off (4)
10. Sparkle (7)
11. Discussions (7)
12. Compact writing method (9)
13. Oust (5)
14. Tightly (7)
15. Position (6)
19. Choral parts (6)
21. Give orders (7)
25. Reinstall (5)
27. Purpose (9)
28. Decorative paper-folding art (7)
29. Full of euphoria (2,1,4)
30. Lack of difficulty (4)
31. Transcriptions (10)

DOWN

1. Consume (6)
2. The masses (3,6)
3. Goes around (7)
4. Usually (8)
5. Highfalutin (2-2-2)
7. Lens opening setting (1-4)
8. Decides (8)
9. Without pride or dignity (6)
16. Food and nourishment (9)
17. Vanquish (8)
18. Genius performer (8)
20. Additions (6)
22. Tall beer mug (7)
23. Separate (6)
24. Moves slowly (6)
26. Does not pass (5)

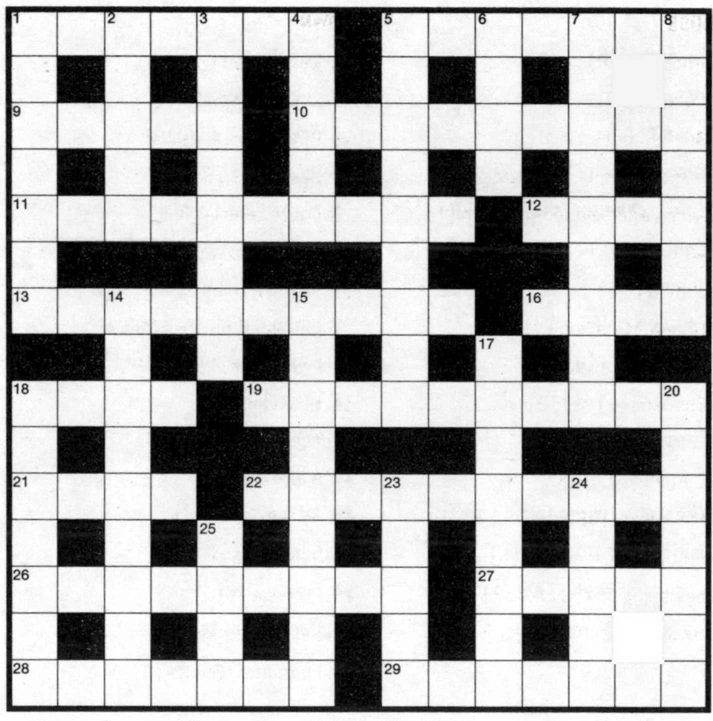

SOLUTION SEE PAGE 242

ACROSS

1. Imagined (7)

5. Possibly (7)

9. Acknowledged (5)

10. Is more significant than (9)

11. A long and severe recession (10)

12. Authentic (4)

13. Junkie (4,6)

16. Breeding stallion (4)

18. Jumps on one leg (4)

19. Space scientist (10)

21. Small devils (4)

22. Curbs (10)

26. Falls down (9)

27. Group of eight things (5)

28. Menacing statements (7)

29. Diva's voice effect (7)

DOWN

1. Deciphered (7)

2. Clear your plate (3,2)

3. Of the Dark Ages (8)

4. Condemns (5)

5. Police vehicle (6,3)

6. Cylinder to wind film onto (4)

7. A set of rules for solving a particular problem (9)

8. Adjourn (7)

14. Not liked (9)

15. Talks about (9)

17. Paper shipping container (8)

18. Coiffure (7)

20. Italian rice dish (7)

23. Propose (5)

24. Get started with gusto (3,2)

25. Computer records (4)

SOLUTION SEE PAGE 242

ACROSS

7. Relish; dressing (5)
8. Really small (4)
9. Rounded and slightly elongated (4)
11. Building to park cars in (6)
12. Unified (8)
13. Gravelly vocal sound (4)
15. Edible fish eggs (3)
16. Wept (5)
19. Acknowledges (7)
20. Unfasten a boat (4,3)
23. Type of black tea (5)
25. Wager (3)
26. Weasel relative (4)
28. Places in front (8)
30. Striking (6)
32. Get wind of (4)
33. Dispatch (4)
34. Individual leaf of paper (5)

DOWN

1. Japanese syllabic writing system (4)
2. Got rid of (8)
3. Social groups (7)
4. Traditional stories (5)
5. Strong aversion (6)
6. Young deer (4)
10. Mysteries (7)
14. Tally (5)
17. Waiflike (5)
18. Between sunrise and sunset (7)
21. The future (8)
22. Ill-treating (7)
24. Special reduced prices (6)
27. Live (5)
29. Was sorry for (4)
31. Make changes (4)

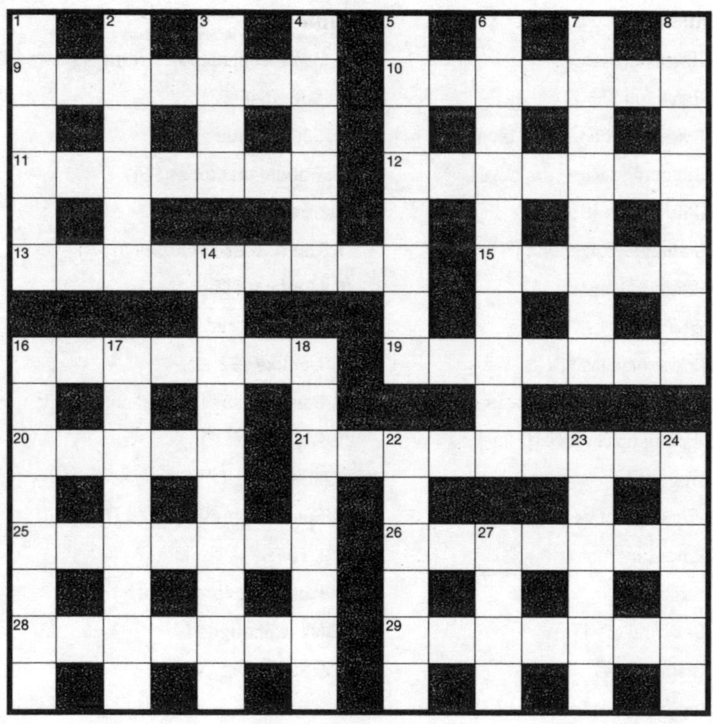

SOLUTION SEE PAGE 243

ACROSS

9. Bizarre (7)

10. Less full (7)

11. Wide strait (7)

12. Lingers (7)

13. Bird scarer (9)

15. Fatuous (5)

16. Dads (7)

19. Pull back (7)

20. Electronic switch (5)

21. Groups of bonded atoms (9)

25. Flying-craft display (3,4)

26. Type of ball rotation (7)

28. Receiver (7)

29. Chapter (7)

DOWN

1. Mentally prepares for a task, with 'up' (6)

2. Fleet of warships (6)

3. Soon, archaically (4)

4. Basement (6)

5. Less brave, informally (8)

6. Upbeat (10)

7. Able to read (8)

8. Potential customer (8)

14. One and all (10)

16. 'Start speaking' (4,4)

17. Bear (8)

18. To a degree (8)

22. Envelope contents? (6)

23. Portable computer (6)

24. Vocalist (6)

27. Settled up (4)

36

SOLUTION SEE PAGE 243

ACROSS

6. Provided food for (7)

7. Seashore (5)

9. Period of 365 days (4)

10. Works out (10)

11. Self-proclaimed moral superior (2-6)

13. Elaborately ornamental style (6)

15. Do as one is told (4)

17. Extracted from the earth (5)

18. Want (4)

19. Admission (6)

20. Nomad (8)

23. Modification (10)

26. Silly person (4)

27. Pilot (5)

28. Buddies (7)

DOWN

1. Common perception (10)

2. Followed (6)

3. Graven image (4)

4. Took place (8)

5. Dad (4)

6. Statement of beliefs (5)

8. Sugar syrup (7)

12. Extend a subscription (5)

14. Changing from one form to another (10)

16. Accumulation (7)

17. Incorrect (8)

21. Pope's envoy (6)

22. Rewrites (5)

24. Islamic chieftain (4)

25. Touch-and-go (4)

SOLUTION SEE PAGE 244

ACROSS

1. Handing over money (6)
4. Found in the sea (6)
9. Short race (4)
10. Inclinations (10)
11. Noble (6)
12. Alternative to metric (8)
13. Heir (9)
15. Alcoholic honey drink (4)
16. Suffering (4)
17. Volume (9)
21. Verdict (8)
22. Full of anxiety (6)
24. Make easier (10)
25. Imprecise (4)
26. Elan (6)
27. Serviceable (6)

DOWN

1. Area of level high ground (7)
2. Rude and noisy person (5)
3. Observes (7)
5. Musical speed reversion (1,5)
6. Wrong (9)
7. Green jewel (7)
8. Ecological (13)
14. Scold (9)
16. Introduction (7)
18. Heads (7)
19. Gentle rain (7)
20. Employing (6)
23. Addict's recovery time (5)

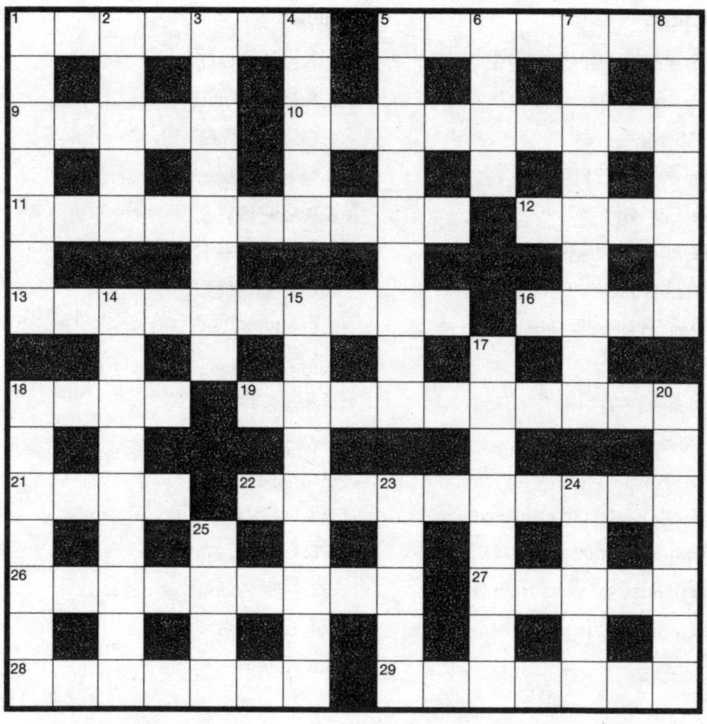

SOLUTION SEE PAGE 244

ACROSS

1. Short spiral pasta (7)
5. Highly detailed (2,5)
9. Kingdom (5)
10. Related to grammar (9)
11. Puts forward (10)
12. Mathematical positions (4)
13. Merry-go-round (10)
16. Air resistance (4)
18. Lash (4)
19. Restraint (10)
21. Retail store (4)
22. Perfectionist (10)
26. Moderate; not excessive (9)
27. Interference pattern (5)
28. Refuse to take part in (7)
29. Animal trainer (7)

DOWN

1. Eternally (7)
2. Stable enclosure (5)
3. Citrus beverage (8)
4. Give out (5)
5. Inflatable hose inside a tyre (5,4)
6. Deceased (4)
7. Dried petal mix (9)
8. Attempting to break into a computer (7)
14. Equally (9)
15. Transmit (9)
17. Amulet (8)
18. Clothes bucket (7)
20. Fusion power type (7)
23. First Hebrew letter (5)
24. Experiment (5)
25. Note (4)

39

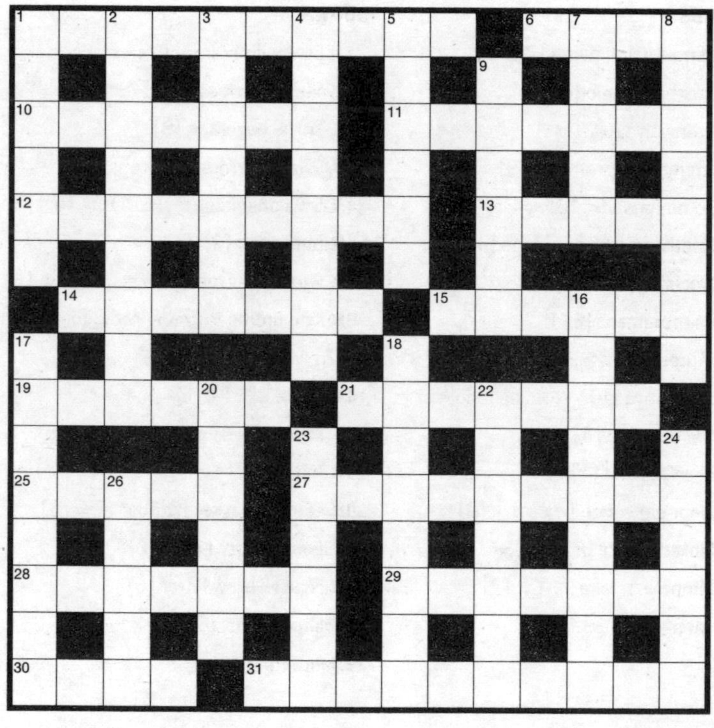

SOLUTION SEE PAGE 245

ACROSS

1. Extra (10)
6. Large wading bird (4)
10. Alternatively (7)
11. Put right (7)
12. Exchanges of differing views (9)
13. Porcelain (5)
14. Proclaim (7)
15. Measurement (6)
19. Expression of approval (6)
21. Flowering plant grown as fodder (7)
25. Musical notes (5)
27. Head honcho (3,6)
28. Inner-ear cavity (7)
29. Table support (7)
30. Tempt (4)
31. Hostile (10)

DOWN

1. Living organism with sensations and voluntary movement (6)
2. Clothing creators (9)
3. Upward current of warm air (7)
4. Commonplace (8)
5. Not moving (2,4)
7. Pancakes served with sour cream (5)
8. Asian food-seasoning liquid (3,5)
9. Frozen water drops (6)
16. Mirrored (9)
17. Done to achieve a specific end (8)
18. Thinner (8)
20. Get comfy against something (6)
22. Sports player (7)
23. Acquire (6)
24. Religious dissent (6)
26. More friendly (5)

SOLUTION SEE PAGE 245

ACROSS

7. Sharp part of a knife (5)
8. Red precious stone (4)
9. Undulating (4)
11. Simple facts (6)
12. Acquiring knowledge (8)
13. Part of an archipelago (4)
15. Overhead shot in tennis (3)
16. Recurring series (5)
19. Estimated (7)
20. Sent out for delivery (7)
23. Provide intellectual instruction (5)
25. Conifer (3)
26. Stand up (4)
28. Pellet gun (3,5)
30. Blown away (6)
32. Departs (4)
33. Acts as an informer (4)
34. Slumbered (5)

DOWN

1. Entreaty (4)
2. Consultants (8)
3. Bedtime song (7)
4. Easily (2,3)
5. A score (6)
6. Cooking range (4)
10. Church book (7)
14. Narrow water inlet (5)
17. Dirty looks (5)
18. While on the contrary (7)
21. Able to run on multiple systems (8)
22. Influences (7)
24. Large wood (6)
27. Blazing, literarily (5)
29. iPhone app symbol (4)
31. Notice (4)

41

SOLUTION SEE PAGE 246

ACROSS

9. Subject of Newton's first law (7)
10. Tomb inscription (7)
11. Victory (7)
12. Imply (7)
13. Public declaration of intent (9)
15. Sort into sequence (5)
16. Pestilences (7)
19. Relating to parody (7)
20. Broad necktie (5)
21. Dismissal of a proposal (9)
25. Mass books (7)
26. Trash (7)
28. Yield (7)
29. Mexican salamander (7)

DOWN

1. One who has suffered harm (6)
2. Quit (6)
3. Extremely small amount (4)
4. Rushes (6)
5. Sittings (8)
6. Analytical (10)
7. Strongly scented purple flower (8)
8. Bombast (8)
14. Thwarted (10)
16. Medical dispensary (8)
17. Blaming (8)
18. Under pressure (8)
22. South American wildcat (6)
23. Back to back (2,1,3)
24. Sewing instrument (6)
27. Large, public brawl (4)

42

SOLUTION SEE PAGE 246

ACROSS

1. Gorges (6)
4. Completely empties (6)
9. Stated (4)
10. Tantamount (10)
11. Miss something out (4,2)
12. Press-gang (8)
13. Valuation (9)
15. Freezes over (4)
16. Culture medium (4)
17. Origin of a word (9)
21. Measures; standards (8)
22. Ethnological (6)
24. Unofficially (10)
25. Wreck (4)
26. Written papers (6)
27. Questioning (6)

DOWN

1. Burst into laughter (5,2)
2. Work out the total (3,2)
3. Distinguished orchestral leaders (7)
5. Uncover (6)
6. Absurd (9)
7. Strapped shoes (7)
8. To a great extent (13)
14. Chemical responses (9)
16. Organize (7)
18. Those killed for religious beliefs (7)
19. Mechanical train (7)
20. Bad-tempered (6)
23. Welsh breed of dog (5)

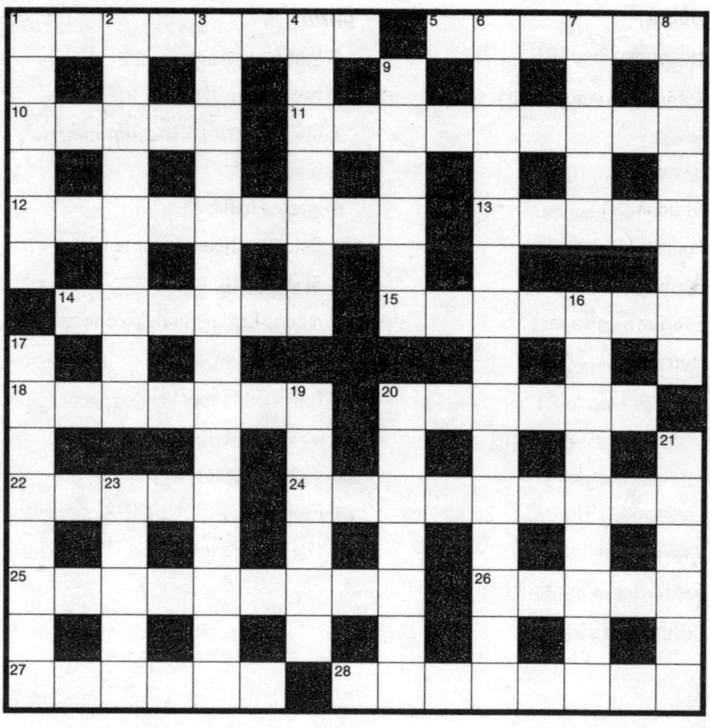

SOLUTION SEE PAGE 247

ACROSS

1. Military leaders (8)
5. Creamy ice cream (6)
10. Allege (5)
11. Owned (9)
12. Residue (9)
13. Teacher (5)
14. Furtive (6)
15. Set-down on paper (7)
18. More horrible (7)
20. Portable (6)
22. Go to the gym, perhaps (5)
24. Spiky tropical fruit (9)
25. Least wide (9)
26. Widely recognized (5)
27. Expression of gratitude (6)
28. Brethren (8)

DOWN

1. Happens (6)
2. Bits (9)
3. Bolt with numbered dials (11,4)
4. Quickly (7)
6. Heated bed cover (8,7)
7. Balance sheet resource (5)
8. Sorting (8)
9. A bond held pending a condition (6)
16. Voice-call device (9)
17. Natural impulse (8)
19. Tore (6)
20. Observe over time (7)
21. Entities (6)
23. Main bodily artery (5)

44

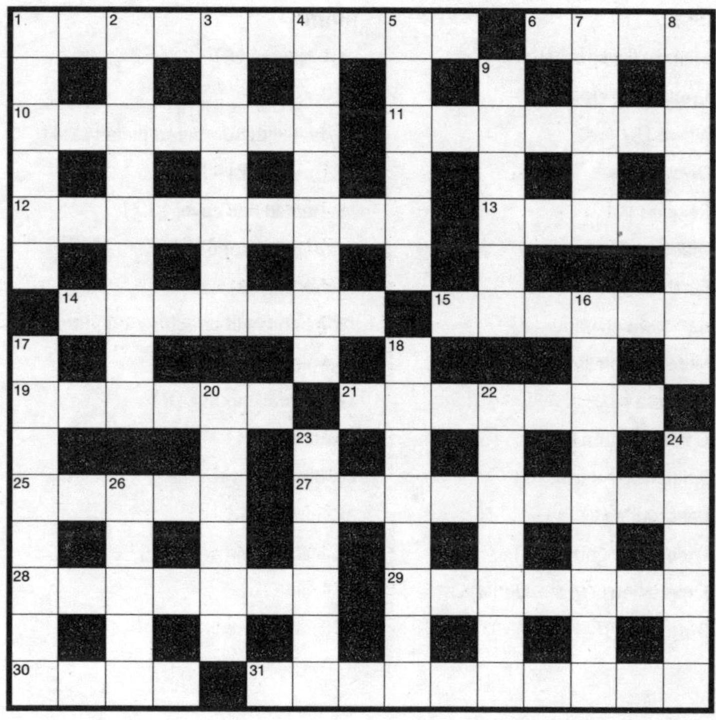

SOLUTION SEE PAGE 247

ACROSS

1. Generally speaking (2,3,5)
6. Aquatic vertebrate (4)
10. Flips over (7)
11. Key finance industry (7)
12. Crackpot (9)
13. Shot from a bow (5)
14. Extend (7)
15. Stupidity (6)
19. Passionate (6)
21. Device for grilling bread (7)
25. Turnabout (5)
27. Replenishes (9)
28. Difficult decision (7)
29. Copy (7)
30. Mythical hairy snow-monster (4)
31. Suffering from great anxiety (10)

DOWN

1. Heated to 100°C (6)
2. Proposed (9)
3. Drive insane (7)
4. Conceptual (8)
5. Retreat (2,4)
7. More glacial (5)
8. Main roads (8)
9. In a continuing forward direction (6)
16. Operating costs (9)
17. Ordinary (3-2-3)
18. Battle (8)
20. A very short moment (2,4)
22. Antiseptic (7)
23. Wild Asian sheep (6)
24. Rise (6)
26. Coastal opening (5)

45

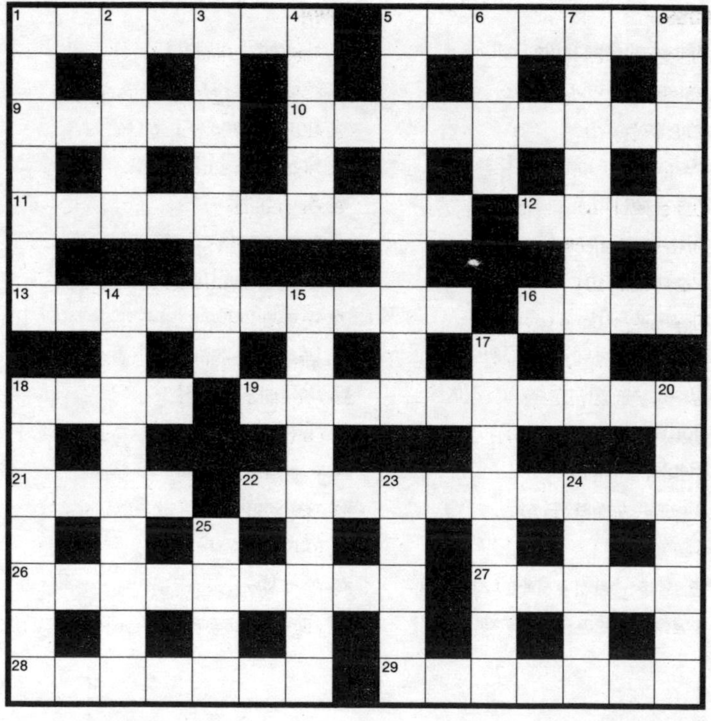

SOLUTION SEE PAGE 248

ACROSS

1. Hold forth (7)
5. Bugs (7)
9. Daft (5)
10. Parted (9)
11. Old-school pharmacist (10)
12. On a single occasion (4)
13. Held back (10)
16. Opposite of cons (4)
18. A hundredth of a euro (4)
19. Bank reports (10)
21. Extended vocal solo (4)
22. Bureaucracy (10)
26. Racing dog (9)
27. Maritime (5)
28. Build in a certain place (7)
29. Puts on clothes (7)

DOWN

1. Feeling of failure (7)
2. Large, stringed instrument (5)
3. At an unknown place (8)
4. Melodious sounds (5)
5. Flawed (9)
6. Baronets (4)
7. Make a hasty escape (3,3,3)
8. Sorrow (7)
14. Tender emotion (9)
15. Acquaint (9)
17. Catholic cardinal (8)
18. Transforms (7)
20. Stops fidgeting (7)
23. Ceased (5)
24. Roof overhangs (5)
25. Flightless South American bird (4)

SOLUTION SEE PAGE 248

ACROSS

7. Woolly ruminant (5)
8. Emotion when in danger (4)
9. Eagerly excited (4)
11. Tour leaders (6)
12. Numerous (8)
13. Spotted-skin disease (4)
15. Army bed (3)
16. Negotiator (5)
19. Male sibling (7)
20. Accord (7)
23. Biochemical test (5)
25. Greek letter 'X' (3)
26. Carry (4)
28. Most fleeting (8)
30. Twine (6)
32. Makes a geographical diagram (4)
33. Religious community member (4)
34. Passing remark (5)

DOWN

1. You (archaic) (4)
2. Tie (4,4)
3. Allows (7)
4. Undoubtedly (5)
5. Feeding (6)
6. Mournful cry (4)
10. Full of anticipation (7)
14. Worries (5)
17. Nine-voice group (5)
18. Least difficult (7)
21. Item for sleeping on (8)
22. Transparent solvent (7)
24. From one side to the other (6)
27. Judges (5)
29. Cure (4)
31. Graph point (4)

47

SOLUTION SEE PAGE 249

ACROSS

6. 1920s decorative style (3,4)
7. Overturn (5)
9. Drinks mixer (4)
10. Commenting on (10)
11. Automated devices (8)
13. Peculiarity (6)
15. Thigh to lower leg joint (4)
17. Reminder notes (5)
18. Just about acceptable (2-2)
19. Grim Reaper's tool? (6)
20. Creates (8)
23. Discusses (10)
26. 'Word' of binary digits (4)
27. Jargon (5)
28. Less dirty (7)

DOWN

1. Appendage (10)
2. Homily (6)
3. Eve's opposite (4)
4. Rebellious (8)
5. Sharp; penetrating (4)
6. Fragrance (5)
8. Gives charitably (7)
12. Conclude a speech (3,2)
14. Upsetting (10)
16. Core (7)
17. Assemblies (8)
21. In the hope of being paid (2,4)
22. Participate (5)
24. Type of language exam (4)
25. Mexican dish (4)

SOLUTION SEE PAGE 249

ACROSS

1. Layered, soft cake (6)
4. Feeling (6)
9. Obstacle (4)
10. A wonderful thing (10)
11. NATO phonetic 'S' (6)
12. Beach water limit (4,4)
13. Wreak havoc on (9)
15. Breezed through (4)
16. Relinquish (4)
17. Set up (9)
21. Bank earnings (8)
22. Completely erase (6)
24. Portable stationery container (6,4)
25. A lecherous gaze (4)
26. Intense beams of light (6)
27. Any country surrounded by water (6)

DOWN

1. Real (7)
2. Large, carnivorous Asian cat (5)
3. Road surface (7)
5. Adequate (6)
6. Selfsame (9)
7. Swamped (7)
8. Even so (2,4,2,2,3)
14. Groups of spectators (9)
16. Not allow to be seen (7)
18. Never dating (7)
19. Follow after (7)
20. Trader (6)
23. Chap, informally (5)

SOLUTION SEE PAGE 250

ACROSS

9. Not good at mixing (7)

10. Take all the profit (5,2)

11. Japanese feudal warrior (7)

12. Imported curios (7)

13. Be deficient (4,5)

15. Simpleton (5)

16. In writing (2,5)

19. Add a point of view (5,2)

20. Scarcer (5)

21. On the whole (2,7)

25. Defrauded (7)

26. Enlarges (7)

28. Change to the opposite direction (7)

29. Not any place (7)

DOWN

1. Compact mountain group (6)

2. Usual (6)

3. Fibster (4)

4. Having white eyes, eg (6)

5. Diverse (8)

6. Testimony (10)

7. Unlimited (8)

8. Sunbed alternative (5,3)

14. Items that keep other things apart (10)

16. Publicly known (2,6)

17. Discern (8)

18. Animal with antlers (8)

22. Infers from various sources (6)

23. Extended (6)

24. Decrease (6)

27. Church benches (4)

50

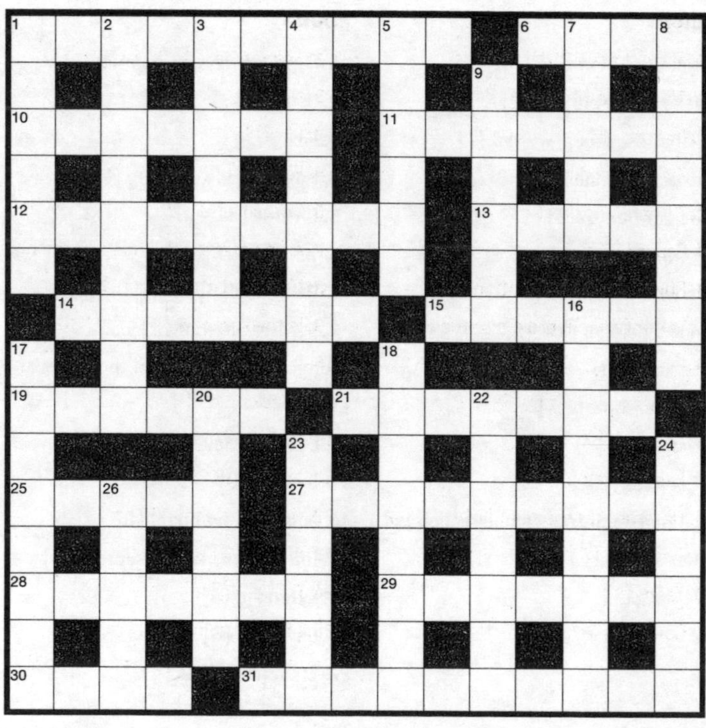

SOLUTION SEE PAGE 250

ACROSS

1. Mirror image (10)
6. Transpose (4)
10. Instructor (7)
11. Finds not guilty (7)
12. Threatening, in chess (9)
13. Caper (5)
14. Row of on-screen buttons (7)
15. Variant chemical arrangement (6)
19. Placed inside another object (6)
21. Weakens; damages (7)
25. Copy and _ (5)
27. Explanation (9)
28. Harmony; agreement (7)
29. Envisage (7)
30. Team (4)
31. Cave dweller (10)

DOWN

1. Solemn ceremony (6)
2. Non-integer numbers (9)
3. Moral (7)
4. Final (8)
5. Citrus fruit (6)
7. Area between the ribs and the hips (5)
8. Unsealed mail item (8)
9. Is the same as (6)
16. Death rate (9)
17. Checks over (8)
18. Taking everything out of (8)
20. An hour before midnight (6)
22. Guacamole ingredient (7)
23. Author (6)
24. Erase (6)
26. Church council (5)

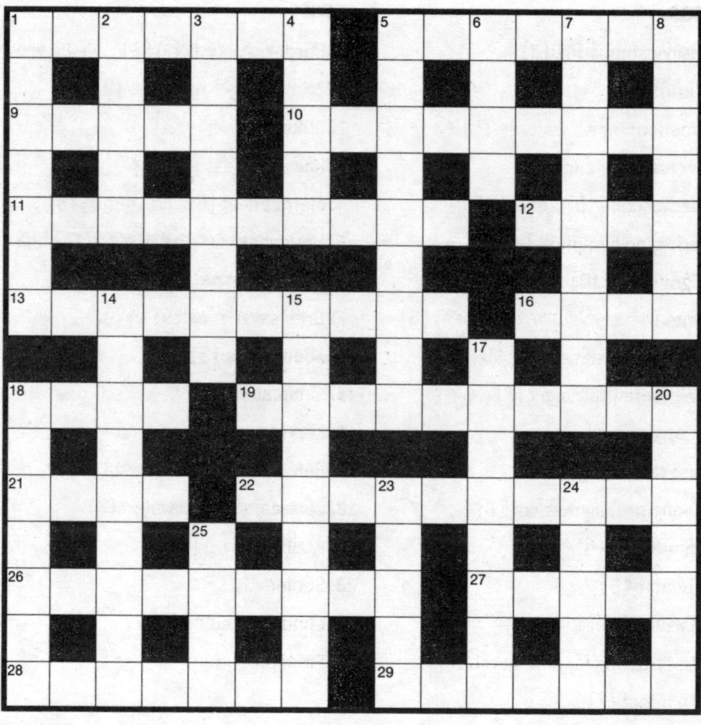

SOLUTION SEE PAGE 251

ACROSS

1. Intoxicating drink (7)
5. Gaffe (4,3)
9. Wooden frames for oxen (5)
10. In respect of (2,7)
11. Methodical (10)
12. Terrifying person (4)
13. Significant (10)
16. Jolts (4)
18. Extinct flightless bird (4)
19. Reinforce (10)
21. Prompted an actor (4)
22. Bird that attacks by swooping downwards (4-6)
26. Went down (9)
27. Opening (5)
28. Marshal (7)
29. Those acting for a monarch who is a minor (7)

DOWN

1. Border plant with small, pale flowers (7)
2. Baked desserts (5)
3. Rampant fear (8)
4. Member of the camel family (5)
5. Household fittings (9)
6. Recommend strongly (4)
7. Brief section of text (9)
8. Female siblings (7)
14. Recipient (9)
15. Learn about (3,4,2)
17. Refusing to take notice of (8)
18. Periods of ten years (7)
20. Apprehensive (7)
23. Senior (5)
24. Conductor's stick (5)
25. Final precursor (4)

52

SOLUTION SEE PAGE 251

ACROSS

7. Type of footwear (5)
8. Kids' spotting game (1,3)
9. Bow notch (4)
11. Bemoan (6)
12. Air is mostly this (8)
13. Egyptian cobras (4)
15. Place to spend the night (3)
16. Olympic decoration (5)
19. Keep going (7)
20. Disobedient, as a child (7)
23. Musical manuscript lines (5)
25. 'That's it!' (3)
26. Spiritual glow (4)
28. Polluted (8)
30. Preference (6)
32. Post-larval insect (4)
33. Small, thin piece of something (4)
34. Fright (5)

DOWN

1. Command to halt a horse (4)
2. Inverts (8)
3. Extremely stupid (7)
4. Bodily sacs (5)
5. No specific people (6)
6. 4,840 square yards (4)
10. To start with (2,5)
14. Perspire (5)
17. Sacrificial block (5)
18. Having the power to do as needed (7)
21. Free ball in soccer (4,4)
22. Most difficult (7)
24. Ocular (6)
27. White outside, perhaps (5)
29. Egg cell (4)
31. Ordinary value (4)

53

SOLUTION SEE PAGE 252

ACROSS

6. Ore (7)

7. Become subject to (5)

9. Remains of a ticket (4)

10. Proscribing (10)

11. Relating to the home (8)

13. Stamen part (6)

15. Small, mosquito-like fly (4)

17. Spare-time activity (5)

18. Skin eruption (4)

19. Pressure (6)

20. Ate (8)

23. Scrapping (10)

26. Parsley or sage (4)

27. Sing like a Tyrolean (5)

28. Having up-to-date knowledge (2,5)

DOWN

1. While not present (2,8)

2. Gain (6)

3. Make indistinct (4)

4. Armed forces in general (8)

5. Decorated, as with a sugary coating (4)

6. Maxim (5)

8. Plasters, as in a wall (7)

12. Involving a third dimension (5)

14. Production rate (10)

16. In particular (7)

17. Truly (8)

21. Periods of darkness (6)

22. Third planet (5)

24. Youths (4)

25. Plant with large, showy flowers (4)

54

SOLUTION SEE PAGE 252

ACROSS

1. Most omniscient (6)

4. Expunges (6)

9. Ticket cost (4)

10. Possessive mark (10)

11. Long-legged cue rest (6)

12. Span (8)

13. This puzzle (9)

15. Taverns (4)

16. Restricted (4)

17. Compatible (9)

21. Obliquely (8)

22. Verse (6)

24. Times after morning (10)

25. Sixty minutes (4)

26. Strata (6)

27. The human mind (6)

DOWN

1. Cover (7)

2. Splash cash, perhaps (5)

3. Type of songbird (7)

5. Sharp reply (6)

6. Abridged (9)

7. Educates (7)

8. Kitchen device (4,9)

14. Honestly (9)

16. Sore (7)

18. Resists (7)

19. Cherish (7)

20. Flag (6)

23. Moral principle (5)

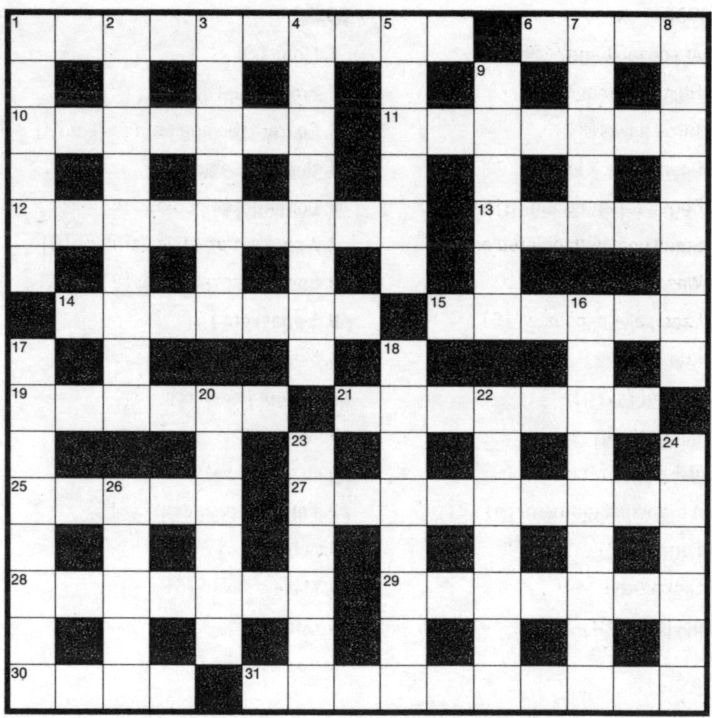

SOLUTION SEE PAGE 253

ACROSS

1. At second hand (10)
6. Hurt or damage (4)
10. Turns down (7)
11. Openly mock (5,2)
12. Physical perception (9)
13. Small boat with pointed ends (5)
14. Was wrong about (7)
15. Lactase or pepsin, eg (6)
19. Rue (6)
21. Intent (7)
25. Conceal (5)
27. The previous century (9)
28. A branch of mathematics (7)
29. Forsake (7)
30. Submissive (4)
31. Jobless (10)

DOWN

1. Flood (6)
2. Protecting (9)
3. Go from the beginning again (7)
4. Unchangeable (4,4)
5. Coming last, perhaps (6)
7. A cook's protective garment (5)
8. Spoke barely audibly (8)
9. Signal light (6)
16. Most recent previous date (9)
17. Announce publicly (8)
18. Tepid (8)
20. Dress in vestments (6)
22. Potential problem (7)
23. Achieve (6)
24. Made a call to (6)
26. Unclear (5)

SOLUTION SEE PAGE 253

ACROSS

9. Culinary herb related to mint (7)
10. Proposition (7)
11. Applies for a reversal of a court decision (7)
12. Snob (7)
13. In addition to (5,4)
15. Thespian (5)
16. Baby toys (7)
19. Agitated (7)
20. Unite (5)
21. In the right place (9)
25. Without artificial additives (7)
26. Improve (7)
28. Three of a kind (7)
29. Biggest (7)

DOWN

1. Classical instrumental composition (6)
2. Do not deviate from (4,2)
3. Crazy (4)
4. Dwarf tree (6)
5. Orations (8)
6. Drugs (10)
7. Pastor (8)
8. Had as a major aspect (8)
14. Basic principle of success (6,4)
16. Meditate (8)
17. Reverse direction and run away (4,4)
18. Nuance (8)
22. At a high volume (6)
23. Pictures (6)
24. Hotel patrons (6)
27. Brace; get ready (4)

57

SOLUTION SEE PAGE 254

ACROSS

7. Wed (5)
8. Drag (4)
9. Wagon (4)
11. Of the mind (6)
12. Lawyer (8)
13. Edible root (4)
15. Black-and-white seabird (3)
16. Farewell (5)
19. Major successes (7)
20. Small, country house (7)
23. Pack full (5)
25. Hit the slopes? (3)
26. Away from the expected course (4)
28. Very thin (8)
30. Inhibition (4-2)
32. Field (4)
33. Chooses, with 'for' (4)
34. Indirectly mocking (5)

DOWN

1. Gardening tool for gathering leaves (4)
2. Formal speeches (8)
3. Bar-based singing activity (7)
4. Woven fabric (5)
5. Tallied (6)
6. Maple or spruce, eg (4)
10. Gratifies (7)
14. Allow to enter (5)
17. Keen (5)
18. This evening (7)
21. Teaching (8)
22. Declares (7)
24. Visual appearance (6)
27. Point of rotation (5)
29. Broadcasts (4)
31. Untie (4)

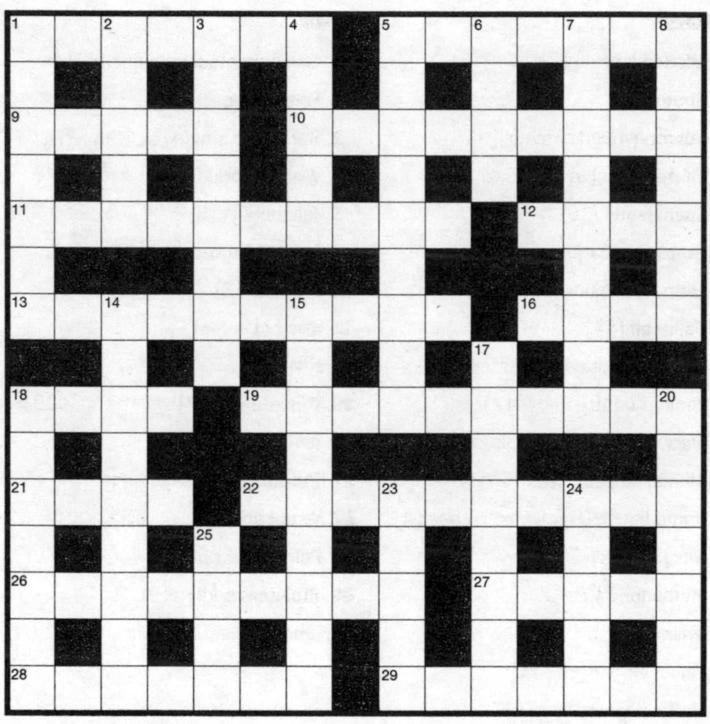

SOLUTION SEE PAGE 254

ACROSS

1. Looked quickly (7)

5. Soothe (7)

9. Poppy-derived narcotic (5)

10. European nobleman (5,4)

11. Speculation (10)

12. Large celebration (4)

13. Formal accusation (10)

16. Daily food (4)

18. Extreme political movement? (4)

19. Concords (10)

21. Smell strongly and unpleasantly (4)

22. Able to be got hold of (10)

26. Immediately (9)

27. Block of gold (5)

28. Methods (7)

29. Not blind (7)

DOWN

1. Italian potato dumplings (7)

2. Bird-related (5)

3. Start (8)

4. Single figure (5)

5. Reschedule (9)

6. Refined woman (4)

7. Imitation (9)

8. Chic (7)

14. Lessens (9)

15. Millions of digital storage units (9)

17. Revising (8)

18. Stretches with great effort (7)

20. Perspired (7)

23. Vast chasm (5)

24. Intolerant person (5)

25. Cause to exist (4)

SOLUTION SEE PAGE 255

ACROSS

1. Obscures (6)

4. Digressions (6)

9. A usually dry water channel (4)

10. Linked (10)

11. Most fresh (6)

12. Tube shape (8)

13. Misgiving (9)

15. Pallid (4)

16. Hang around (4)

17. Self-important display (9)

21. Cabbage relative (8)

22. Fable (6)

24. Overly trivialized (10)

25. Ethereal (4)

26. Oily (6)

27. Hymn (6)

DOWN

1. French castle (7)

2. Chilled (2,3)

3. Severe (7)

5. Corn-cutting tool (6)

6. Medical analysis (9)

7. Background landscape (7)

8. Brain scientists (13)

14. Fundamental law (9)

16. Functioning (7)

18. Large-billed waterbird (7)

19. Cut-paper puzzle (7)

20. Animal frames (6)

23. Grind teeth (5)

SOLUTION SEE PAGE 255

ACROSS

6. Calamity (7)
7. Inclines (5)
9. Slender, tubular instrument (4)
10. Experts on the past (10)
11. Student assignment (8)
13. Skip over (6)
15. Photo (4)
17. Loud, jarring sound (5)
18. Provoke (4)
19. Beer container (6)
20. Ceremonial act of self-washing (8)
23. Falling share prices (4,6)
26. Wheel shaft (4)
27. Stories (5)
28. Own (7)

DOWN

1. Doorman (10)
2. Electronic dance genre (6)
3. Nays' opposites (4)
4. Granting (8)
5. Silk garment worn draped around the body (4)
6. Off-limits through social convention (5)
8. Spanish punch (7)
12. Eucalyptus-eater (5)
14. Discussed (10)
16. Least distance way (7)
17. Flop (8)
21. Newest (6)
22. Gawks at (5)
24. Character; part (4)
25. Retained (4)

61

SOLUTION SEE PAGE 256

ACROSS

9. Set apart (7)

10. Coincide (7)

11. Adult (5-2)

12. Learns about (7)

13. Withdrawn (9)

15. Gold star, eg (5)

16. Much feared (7)

19. Blushes (7)

20. Bounteous (5)

21. Formal procedures (9)

25. Contact (7)

26. Tossed (7)

28. Physics, eg (7)

29. Round part in the human vision system (7)

DOWN

1. Small laugh (6)

2. Exit gracefully (3,3)

3. Sign of boredom (4)

4. Brewing crockery (6)

5. Think (8)

6. Energy (3-2-3-2)

7. Final (8)

8. Chapters (8)

14. Speaking to (10)

16. Complete lack of success (4,4)

17. Stress (8)

18. Relied (8)

22. Make up for (6)

23. Parentless child (6)

24. Bicycle seat (6)

27. The _ of March (4)

SOLUTION SEE PAGE 256

ACROSS

7. Specks (5)

8. Crawl (4)

9. Adonis (4)

11. Air inlet (6)

12. Seen (8)

13. Adhesive (4)

15. Writing fluid (3)

16. Requested (5)

19. Extremely large (7)

20. Photographic equipment (7)

23. Regular (5)

25. Stick out (3)

26. Equal in score (4)

28. Type of guitar (8)

30. Golf-ball hit (6)

32. Sprint contest (4)

33. Allow access to (4)

34. Not yet written on (5)

DOWN

1. Connect (4)

2. Bosses (8)

3. Unlatches (7)

4. Elected (5)

5. Enchants (6)

6. Poker stake (4)

10. Accept (7)

14. Debts (5)

17. Uplift (5)

18. Dream (7)

21. Wholly (8)

22. Thrown out (7)

24. Makes laugh (6)

27. Endured (5)

29. Common crustacean (4)

31. Nice to other people (4)

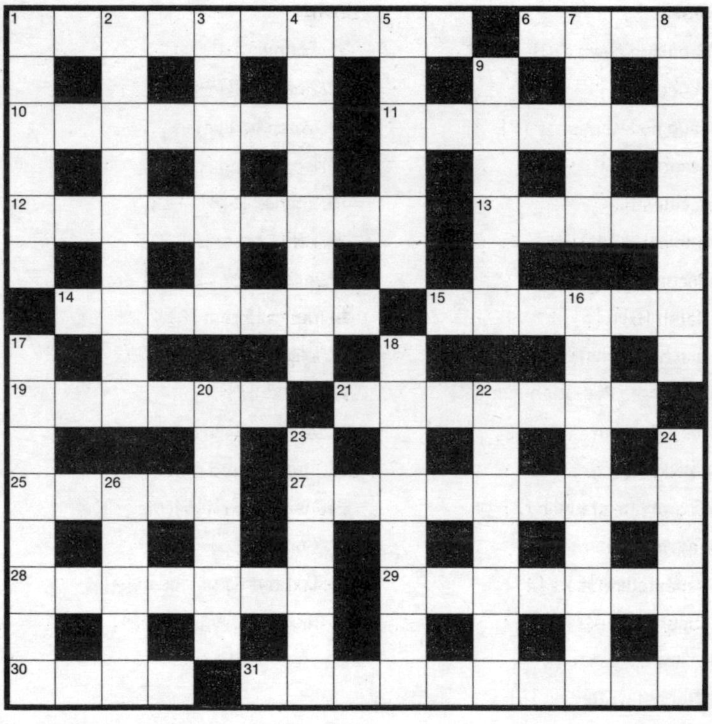

SOLUTION SEE PAGE 257

ACROSS

1. Breaking down (10)
6. Peaceful (4)
10. Pays no attention to (7)
11. Game token (7)
12. Accidentally (2,7)
13. Tropical lizard (5)
14. Occurring (7)
15. Harsh (6)
19. Touched with the lips (6)
21. Vindicate (7)
25. Dismiss from a job (3,2)
27. Liked better (9)
28. End-of-line stations (7)
29. Leaving (7)
30. Repeated refusals (4)
31. Supports (10)

DOWN

1. Ascends (6)
2. Recognizable features (9)
3. Takes into custody (7)
4. Keeps going (8)
5. Notched (6)
7. Loft (5)
8. Besides (8)
9. Tropical forest (6)
16. Obliging compliance (9)
17. Human bones (8)
18. Self-critical conscience (8)
20. Out of the ordinary (6)
22. Even more minuscule (7)
23. Choice (6)
24. Maxims (6)
26. Trinity (5)

64

SOLUTION SEE PAGE 257

ACROSS

1. Desktop arrow (6)

4. Allows entry (6)

9. Hair arranger (4)

10. Conversion process (10)

11. Bathing top and bottoms (6)

12. Least old (8)

13. Natural consumption cycle (4,5)

15. Den (4)

16. Female relative (4)

17. Tactical (9)

21. As a response (2,6)

22. Busy; energetic (6)

24. Servile flattery (10)

25. Supreme beings (4)

26. Want (6)

27. Situation (6)

DOWN

1. Spicy pork sausage (7)

2. Jewish scholar (5)

3. Large, flightless bird (7)

5. Athletic throwing event (6)

6. Merge together (9)

7. Commercial backer (7)

8. Laid-back popular music (4,9)

14. Perilous (9)

16. Bothered (7)

18. Financial researcher (7)

19. Infiltrates (7)

20. Writer (6)

23. Taut (5)

65

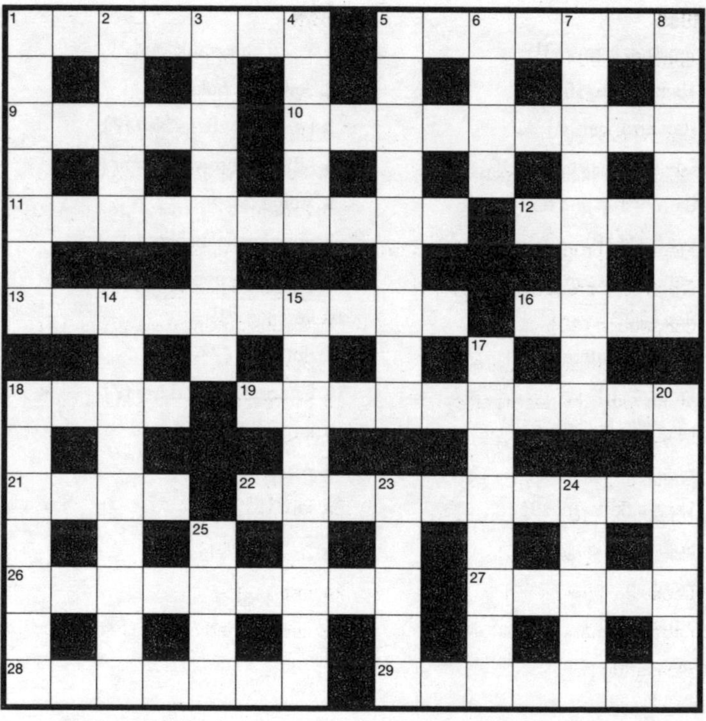

SOLUTION SEE PAGE 258

ACROSS

1. Concentrated (7)

5. Boring (7)

9. Dutch bulb (5)

10. Relating to the process of governing (9)

11. Electricity producing machines (10)

12. Fresh-food products counter (4)

13. Commotion (10)

16. Corrode with acid (4)

18. Atoms with net electric charge (4)

19. Increase in speed (10)

21. Consisting of two parts (4)

22. Nominees (10)

26. Hundreds of years (9)

27. Chocolate powder (5)

28. Caustic remark (7)

29. Pleasantly (7)

DOWN

1. Extreme tiredness (7)

2. Punctuation mark (5)

3. Divided (8)

4. Warehouse (5)

5. Permitted degree of variation (9)

6. Appointment (4)

7. Large musical group (9)

8. Always putting oneself first (7)

14. Box (9)

15. System of parts in a machine (9)

17. Cranial pain (8)

18. Brings on (7)

20. Great joy (7)

23. Drug quantities (5)

24. Implied (5)

25. Low-pitched musical instrument (4)

66

SOLUTION SEE PAGE 258

ACROSS

6. Greeting (7)
7. Make a change to (5)
9. Blood circulation tube (4)
10. Unequivocal (10)
11. Nuclear weapon (4,4)
13. Fast food item (3,3)
15. Check for irregularities (4)
17. Actor's parts (5)
18. Of the same type (4)
19. Alludes (6)
20. Forebear (8)
23. Decorative art style (3,7)
26. Nocturnal birds of prey (4)
27. Holy memento (5)
28. Supposed (7)

DOWN

1. Sweet milk dessert (10)
2. Black magic (6)
3. Shorten, as in a sail (4)
4. Sets a ship afloat (8)
5. 'Right away!', in hospital (4)
6. Type of cereal plant (5)
8. Pasta envelopes (7)
12. Corkwood (5)
14. Changes (10)
16. Less cloudy (7)
17. Asset (8)
21. Route (6)
22. Stared at longingly (5)
24. Having no legally binding power, as a contract (4)
25. Brio (4)

SOLUTION SEE PAGE 259

ACROSS

7. Threads (5)
8. Bay (4)
9. Ship body (4)
11. Diversion (6)
12. Paid attention to a sound (8)
13. Flightless bird (4)
15. Involuntary drunken sound (3)
16. Off the cuff (2,3)
19. Pardon (7)
20. Porch (7)
23. Mentally prepare; excite (5)
25. Master (3)
26. Metal containers (4)
28. Achievements (8)
30. Without difficulty (6)
32. Possess (4)
33. Small valley (4)
34. Fits one inside another (5)

DOWN

1. Title (4)
2. Encryption (8)
3. Assemble (7)
4. Fewest (5)
5. Protect from danger (6)
6. Duct for smoke (4)
10. Document repository (7)
14. Popular heroes (5)
17. Relating to bygone times, archaically (5)
18. Transitions into (7)
21. Opened, as a computer file (8)
22. Biblical letter (7)
24. Bingo announcer (6)
27. Air currents (5)
29. Bag examination (1-3)
31. Does not forbid (4)

SOLUTION SEE PAGE 259

ACROSS

1. Illicit wall drawings (8)

5. Consented (6)

10. Respond to an enquiry (5)

11. Deductions (9)

12. Honorific, as in a title (2,7)

13. One having lunch, perhaps (5)

14. Small firearm (6)

15. Rivers (7)

18. The most large (7)

20. Real (6)

22. "Carmen", eg (5)

24. Sent to the printer, perhaps (9)

25. Trademark (5,4)

26. Elector (5)

27. Considered (6)

28. Draws in (8)

DOWN

1. Cultivated area (6)

2. Sanctioning (9)

3. Blow a fuse, perhaps (3,3,3,6)

4. Average (7)

6. Large dog with dark-cream hair (6,9)

7. Expel (5)

8. Great sorrow (8)

9. Vexes (6)

16. Indifferent (9)

17. Engrossed (8)

19. Tall, cylindrical headwear (3,3)

20. Surrounding (7)

21. Idolizes (6)

23. Obliterate (5)

69

SOLUTION SEE PAGE 260

ACROSS

9. Large deer (7)
10. The study of living organisms (7)
11. Extents (7)
12. Persecute (7)
13. Continually self-referencing (9)
15. Frosting (5)
16. Bike rider (7)
19. Primary constituent of matter (7)
20. Visitors to a website (5)
21. Intermediate (2-7)
25. Violent windstorm (7)
26. Highly strung (7)
28. Genuine (7)
29. Dismissal (5-2)

DOWN

1. Connected with vision (6)
2. Wry (6)
3. Adjoin (4)
4. Mixed cereal breakfast (6)
5. Out of date (8)
6. Praise (10)
7. On an unspecified date (8)
8. Ability to see (8)
14. Restored (10)
16. Politeness (8)
17. Treeless forest area (8)
18. Fitted to size, as clothes (8)
22. Purchased (6)
23. Less at ease (6)
24. Country (6)
27. Defrost (4)

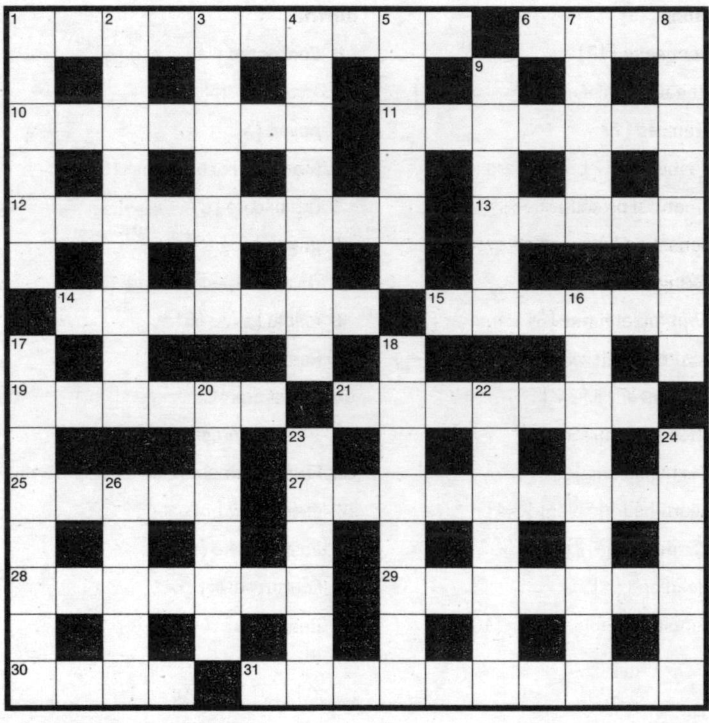

SOLUTION SEE PAGE 260

ACROSS

1. Sequence (10)
6. Imitated (4)
10. Frenzied (7)
11. Pushes suddenly forward (7)
12. Financial protection (9)
13. Sensation; unexpected event (5)
14. Young child (7)
15. Kept for later use (6)
19. Type of edible nut (6)
21. Abducts (7)
25. Neat and tidy (5)
27. Permissible (9)
28. Acorn-bearing plant (3,4)
29. Condemning (7)
30. Headland (4)
31. Popular primula variety (10)

DOWN

1. Word ending (6)
2. Place of learning (9)
3. Input (7)
4. Endorsed (8)
5. The start of something (6)
7. Linguine, eg (5)
8. Throws away (8)
9. Assets (6)
16. Print again (9)
17. Retreat from a decision (4,4)
18. Military exercise (5,3)
20. Authorized document certifier (6)
22. Maternity-ward baby (7)
23. Become fond of (4,2)
24. Melds together (6)
26. Creates (5)

SOLUTION SEE PAGE 261

ACROSS

1. Planetarium (6)

4. Beaded counting tool (6)

9. Afresh; another time (4)

10. At the same temperature (10)

11. Socialize with those of higher status (6)

12. Hidden (8)

13. Aircraft control system (3-2-4)

15. At the summit of (4)

16. Palaver (4)

17. Biblical writings that aren't canon (9)

21. Indian ruler's wife, historically (8)

22. Consecrate a priest (6)

24. Ahead of time (10)

25. Codeword for 'E' (4)

26. Flora (6)

27. Those older than children (6)

DOWN

1. Score against yourself, in soccer (3,4)

2. Mountain ash (5)

3. Prism display (7)

5. Personal request (6)

6. Electronic components (9)

7. Develop in a promising way (5,2)

8. Realistic, as landscapes in art (13)

14. Samba relative (5,4)

16. Sudden outburst (5-2)

18. Packed (7)

19. Elevations (7)

20. Warning (6)

23. Reside (5)

SOLUTION SEE PAGE 261

ACROSS

7. Remembrance flower (5)

8. Tight; close-fitting (4)

9. Shielded recess (4)

11. Small racing vehicle (2-4)

12. Singularly (8)

13. Hired transport vehicle (4)

15. Comic screech (3)

16. Student bar orders (5)

19. Underwater eye protection (7)

20. Communicates with gestures (7)

23. Swimming pool statistic (5)

25. Distant (3)

26. Message sent to a phone (4)

28. Propose (8)

30. Child's glove without individual fingers (6)

32. Be wide open (4)

33. Spouse (4)

34. Treat (5)

DOWN

1. Fuss (2-2)

2. Applying changes (8)

3. Jinxed (7)

4. Another time (5)

5. Give rise to (6)

6. Work hard (4)

10. Drove a car (7)

14. Overhead (5)

17. Unwind (5)

18. Model landscape scene (7)

21. Writing system (8)

22. Results (7)

24. Clans (6)

27. Heats up (5)

29. Adequate (4)

31. Whirling mist (4)

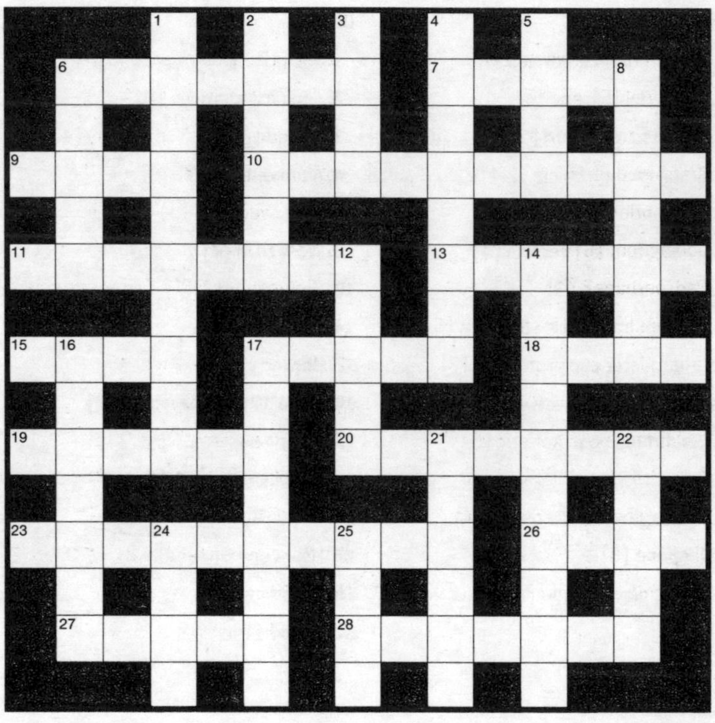

SOLUTION SEE PAGE 262

ACROSS

6. Tentacled underwater feeder (7)
7. Municipal (5)
9. Middle Eastern hors d'oeuvre dishes (4)
10. Restrained (10)
11. Indian prince (8)
13. Sloping font (6)
15. iPad, perhaps? (4)
17. Type of keyboard instrument (5)
18. Satisfy (4)
19. Happenings (6)
20. Avalanche, eg (8)
23. Eager interest (10)
26. Biblical ships (4)
27. Disgrace (5)
28. Microchip element (7)

DOWN

1. Surprising disclosure (10)
2. 'You fell for it!' (6)
3. Used in fluorescent lamps (4)
4. Zodiac creature (8)
5. Very, very bad (4)
6. Sphere of activity (5)
8. Compounds and substances scientist (7)
12. Heavenly messenger (5)
14. Support (10)
16. Comes up with (7)
17. Preoccupies (8)
21. That is to say (6)
22. Make permanent (3,2)
24. Cranium (4)
25. Plus (4)

74

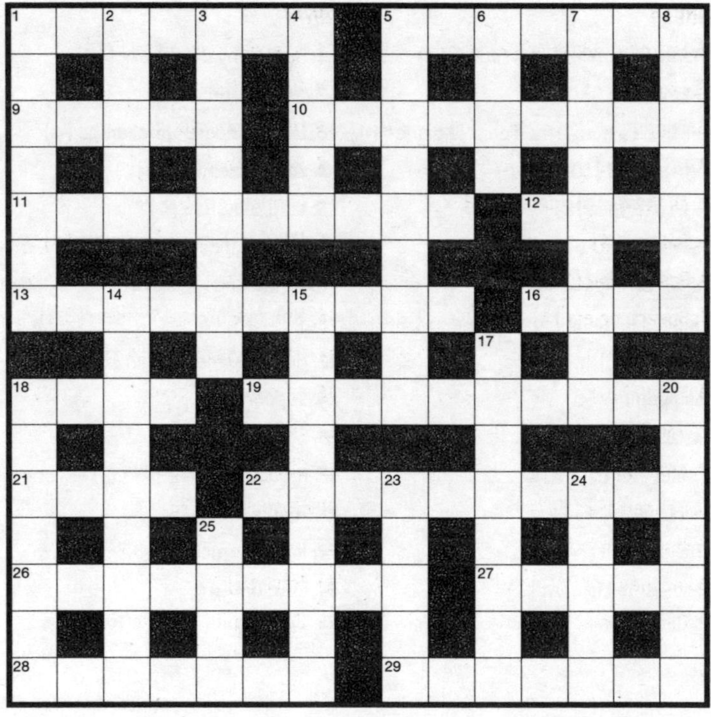

SOLUTION SEE PAGE 262

ACROSS

1. Erupting mountain (7)
5. Fixed (7)
9. Funny (5)
10. In an accurate manner (9)
11. As the real person (2,3,5)
12. Tail end (4)
13. Resignation (10)
16. Speech defect (4)
18. Entrance (4)
19. Fervid (10)
21. Helps (4)
22. Aroused (10)
26. Defined (9)
27. Tomb (5)
28. Inclined (7)
29. Disfigures (7)

DOWN

1. Affected individuals (7)
2. Boundary (5)
3. Officially certify (8)
4. Butcher's leftovers (5)
5. Forefathers (9)
6. Flightless Australian birds (4)
7. Hedonism (5,4)
8. Non-overnight excursion (3,4)
14. Large, edible, flat green legume (5,4)
15. Astounding (9)
17. Thug (8)
18. Strongly committed (4,3)
20. Unceasing (7)
23. Internet-provider device (5)
24. Track (5)
25. Community website (4)

75

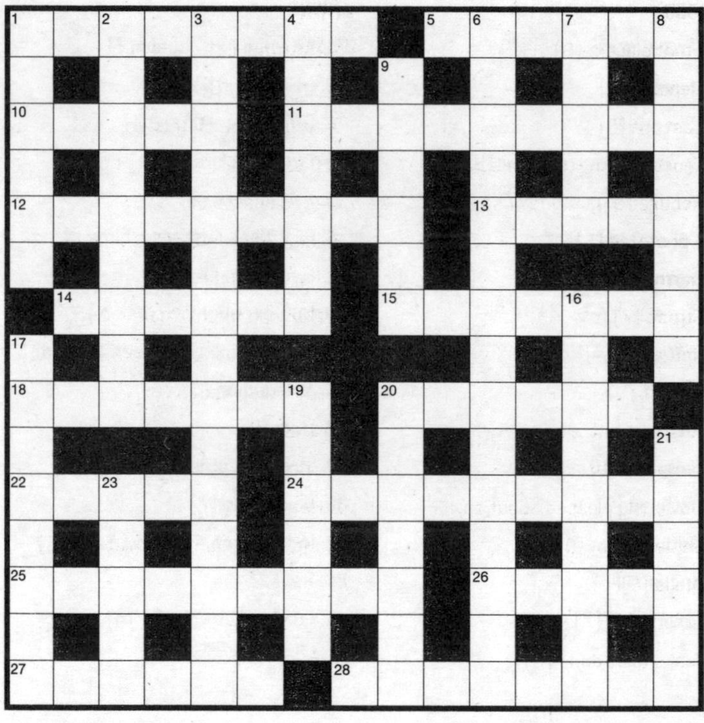

SOLUTION SEE PAGE 263

ACROSS

1. Front players (8)

5. Repeats (6)

10. Cast out (5)

11. Those starting to learn a skill (9)

12. Rebuke (5,4)

13. A photo, eg (5)

14. Narrow boats (6)

15. Strode (7)

18. Refuge (7)

20. Safe (6)

22. Abscond with a lover (5)

24. Gorgeous (9)

25. Obviously pleased about an achievement (4-1-4)

26. Atolls (5)

27. Squirts (6)

28. Tasks to be done (8)

DOWN

1. Pastures (6)

2. Say again (9)

3. Association method for giving up (8,7)

4. Doubtful (7)

6. Type of swindle (10,5)

7. Last Greek letter (5)

8. Bars temporarily (8)

9. 007 and friends? (6)

16. Collected body of work (9)

17. Intrinsic natures (8)

19. Decoration for a present (6)

20. Soap for washing your hair (7)

21. Not open (6)

23. Type of aquarium cichlid fish (5)

76

SOLUTION SEE PAGE 263

ACROSS

1. Goal (6)
4. Prepare, as in plans (4,2)
9. Profit (4)
10. Quarrelsome (10)
11. Noisy grass insect (6)
12. Doctrine (8)
13. Joy (9)
15. Row of seats (4)
16. Voucher; receipt (4)
17. Extremely sick (2,1,3,3)
21. Advocate of women's rights (8)
22. Being (6)
24. Gets in the way (10)
25. Snare (4)
26. Intensely (6)
27. A chocoholic, eg (6)

DOWN

1. Egg-shaped wind instrument (7)
2. Government after a coup (5)
3. Team leader (7)
5. Book user (6)
6. Tornado (9)
7. Sink unblocker (7)
8. Artificially forced (7,6)
14. Special right (9)
16. Removed dirt (7)
18. Sanctified (7)
19. Entice (7)
20. Wicked (6)
23. As one, in music (5)

77

SOLUTION SEE PAGE 264

ACROSS

7. This date (5)
8. Astound (4)
9. Industrial fair (4)
11. As much as can be held (6)
12. Participating (8)
13. Vegetarian ingredient (4)
15. It's laid by a bird (3)
16. Look forward to (5)
19. Common ocean-side bird (7)
20. Grasp; understand (5,2)
23. Literary work (5)
25. Female chicken (3)
26. Type of gemstone (4)
28. Prone to an unwanted medical reaction (8)
30. Provide (6)
32. Membership fees (4)
33. Wine sediment (4)
34. Readily available (2,3)

DOWN

1. Rain heavily (4)
2. Widely distributed (3-5)
3. Violins and cellos (7)
4. Rogue (5)
5. Fade with age (6)
6. Blunted fencing weapon (4)
10. Old (7)
14. Auguries (5)
17. Wryly amusing contradictions (5)
18. Insanity (7)
21. Axing (8)
22. Proofreader (7)
24. Not inclined (6)
27. Spry (5)
29. Aggressive man (4)
31. Jump over (4)

78

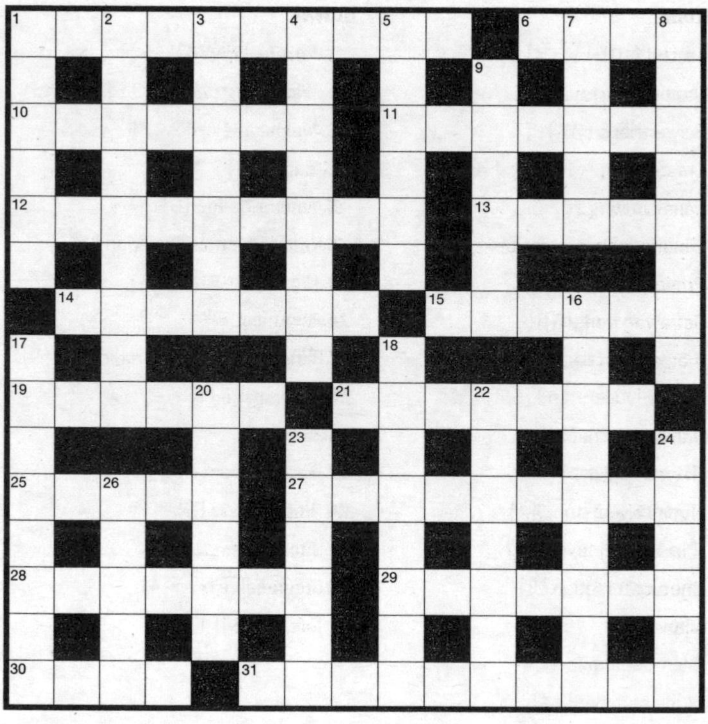

SOLUTION SEE PAGE 264

ACROSS

1. Tactful (10)
6. Jazz singing style (4)
10. Screenplays (7)
11. Create (7)
12. Calms down (9)
13. Luxurious Roman residence (5)
14. Provokes (7)
15. Get away from (6)
19. Indigenous (6)
21. Gather (7)
25. Subsidiary theorem in a proof (5)
27. Oversaw (9)
28. Not as big (7)
29. Friendly (7)
30. Chutzpah (4)
31. Aliens (10)

DOWN

1. Barren place (6)
2. Everlasting (9)
3. Against (7)
4. Mixed (8)
5. Appoint by force (6)
7. Nasty (5)
8. Juvenile person (8)
9. Figures out (6)
16. Praiseworthy (9)
17. Investigation (8)
18. Cut short (8)
20. Workable; possible (6)
22. On a chair, eg (7)
23. Unborn offspring (6)
24. Goodbyes (6)
26. Intends (5)

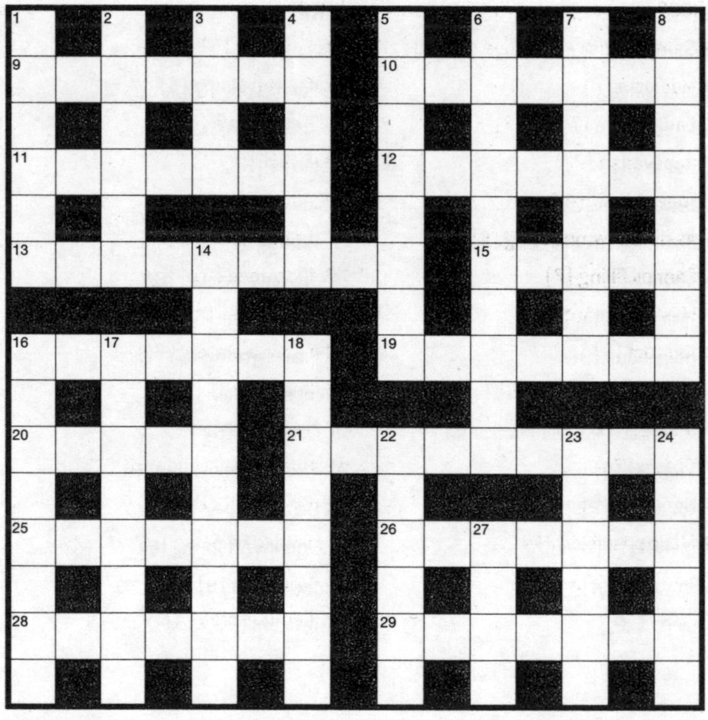

SOLUTION SEE PAGE 265

ACROSS

9. Stores with a wide range of goods (7)
10. Mediocre (7)
11. Land area measure (7)
12. Impoverish (7)
13. Type of knot (4,5)
15. Assists in wrongdoing (5)
16. Cannoli filling (7)
19. Mass celebrants (7)
20. Instruct (5)
21. Machine designers (9)
25. Disregarded (7)
26. Obtain (7)
28. Brave; courageous (7)
29. Made possible (7)

DOWN

1. Separate (6)
2. Curved shape (6)
3. Killer whale (4)
4. Gift (6)
5. Adversity (8)
6. Enticement (10)
7. Indolence (8)
8. Publishes (8)
14. Leave a place (3,3,4)
16. Recover (8)
17. TV options (8)
18. Humorous account (8)
22. Crushed rocks (6)
23. Safe to be eaten (6)
24. Velocities (6)
27. Campus area (4)

80

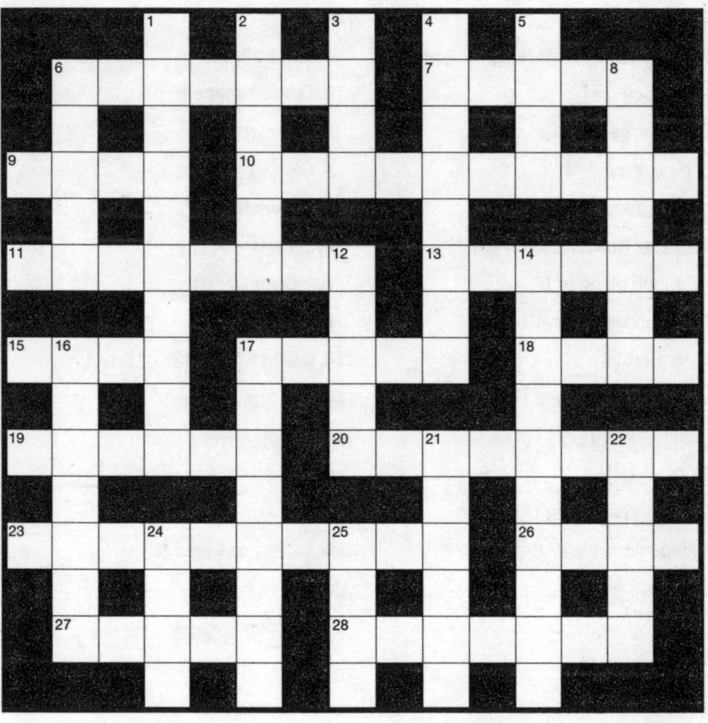

SOLUTION SEE PAGE 265

ACROSS

6. Dawn (7)

7. Recorded (5)

9. Remove the skin from (4)

10. Business initiative (10)

11. Unicellular organisms (8)

13. Smoothed some shirts, perhaps (6)

15. Allied countries (4)

17. Seeking damages (5)

18. Terminates (4)

19. Spanish dish cooked in a shallow pan (6)

20. Keeps busy (8)

23. Place of secondary education (4,6)

26. Individual account entry (4)

27. Hand covering (5)

28. General idea (7)

DOWN

1. Diagnostic (10)

2. One-dimensional (6)

3. Marquee (4)

4. Rousing (8)

5. Stout pole on a ship (4)

6. Inscribed column (5)

8. Move down (7)

12. Mexican friend (5)

14. Too expensive (10)

16. At the front (7)

17. Looked (8)

21. New emigrant settlement (6)

22. Choose (5)

24. Head covering (4)

25. Cry of pain (4)

81

SOLUTION SEE PAGE 266

ACROSS

1. Common type of dove (6)
4. Delay (4-2)
9. Musical movement (4)
10. Basis (10)
11. Like a movie (6)
12. Hassles (8)
13. Contemplating (9)
15. Took advantage of (4)
16. Heavy book, perhaps (4)
17. Right now (2,7)
21. Artistic setting (8)
22. Turmoils (6)
24. Very fashionable (3,3,4)
25. Rows a boat (4)
26. Debt or obligation evader (6)
27. Also (2,4)

DOWN

1. Elaborate, columned porch (7)
2. Man marrying a bride (5)
3. One in a position of authority (7)
5. Probable (4-2)
6. Information repositories (9)
7. Continue (7)
8. Involving several countries (13)
14. Had power and influence over (9)
16. Made an attempt to deal with (7)
18. Duty rolls (7)
19. Digit (7)
20. Gentle wind (6)
23. Endangered atmosphere layer (5)

82

SOLUTION SEE PAGE 266

ACROSS

7. Female gonad, medically (5)

8. Prune (4)

9. Circular track (4)

11. Large concert venues (6)

12. User (8)

13. Make a jumper, perhaps (4)

15. Wipe back and forth (3)

16. Michaelmas daisy genus (5)

19. Elixir (4-3)

20. Bundle (7)

23. Accepted practice (5)

25. Is endowed with (3)

26. Solemn promise (4)

28. Look after (8)

30. Bothering (6)

32. Large-winged nocturnal insect (4)

33. Skeletal (4)

34. Not competent (5)

DOWN

1. Always (4)

2. Having brown hair (8)

3. Open to question (2,5)

4. Anxious; worried (5)

5. Purifies (6)

6. Game played on horseback (4)

10. Generally speaking (2,1,4)

14. Words used to identify things (5)

17. Two cubed (5)

18. Christmas toast (7)

21. Rapping (8)

22. Giving out light (7)

24. Zealously enthusiastic (4-2)

27. Ballroom dance that originated in Brazil (5)

29. Aftersun treatment (4)

31. Pinches; squeezes (4)

83

SOLUTION SEE PAGE 267

ACROSS

1. Investigated (10)
6. Arthritic disease (4)
10. Rejection (7)
11. Equity (7)
12. Fabled (9)
13. Strong feeling of annoyance (5)
14. In the past (7)
15. Relating to cats (6)
19. Flat-bladed oar (6)
21. Sleeping chamber (7)
25. A certain punctuation mark (5)
27. Commemorate (9)
28. Chemical symbols equation (7)
29. First name abbreviation (7)
30. Large, round container (4)
31. Scared (10)

DOWN

1. Almost never (6)
2. Protect (9)
3. Military store (7)
4. Gathers together, as in information (8)
5. Relishes (6)
7. Unpaid (5)
8. Hypotheses (8)
9. All your money and possessions (6)
16. Separation (9)
17. Particular (8)
18. Answering (8)
20. Group of competing teams (6)
22. Constructed again (7)
23. Cream-filled cake (6)
24. Securely closed (6)
26. Bogs down (5)

84

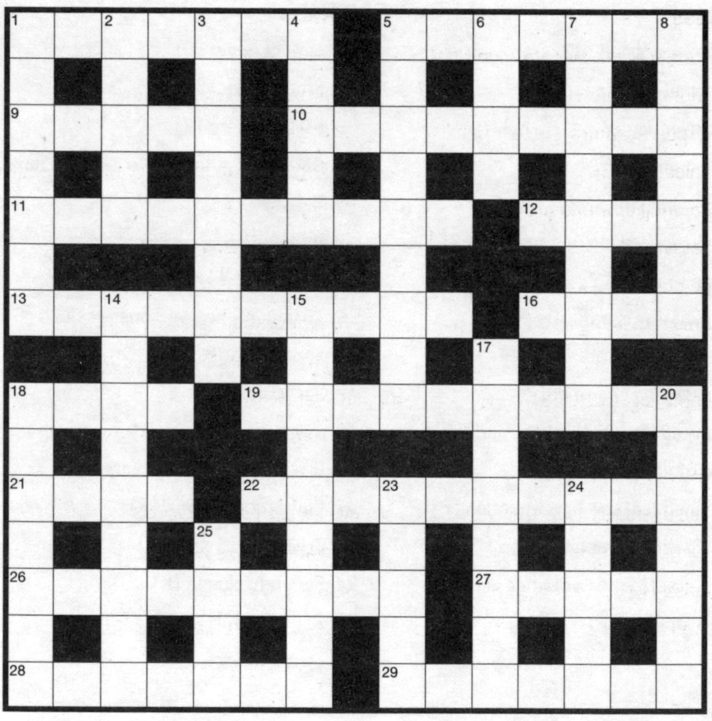

SOLUTION SEE PAGE 267

ACROSS

1. Former Greek monetary unit (7)
5. Triumph (7)
9. Airport scanning system (5)
10. Colonizes (9)
11. Pointing upwards (10)
12. Release (4)
13. Removed minor details (10)
16. Only remaining (4)
18. If not (4)
19. Come together (5,5)
21. Break in the action (4)
22. Offensive action (10)
26. Receivers (9)
27. Iron, eg (5)
28. Asian (7)
29. Puts in (7)

DOWN

1. Deduces (7)
2. Small, poisonous snake (5)
3. Ghastly (8)
4. Dominant animal in a pack (5)
5. Providers (9)
6. Shout out a name (4)
7. Amuse (9)
8. Believe to be guilty (7)
14. Positions incorrectly (9)
15. Mature (4-5)
17. Takes for granted (8)
18. Magnify (7)
20. One-on-one tennis (7)
23. Swiss grated-potatoes dish (5)
24. Bury (5)
25. Semicircular projection from a building (4)

85

SOLUTION SEE PAGE 268

ACROSS

6. Body of troops (7)

7. Secret lover (5)

9. Finely chopped meat and veg dish (4)

10. Beneficial (10)

11. Wedge to keep an entrance open (8)

13. Visual appeal (6)

15. Summit of a hill (4)

17. Once and then again (5)

18. Nonsense (4)

19. Slim and elegant (6)

20. Backpack (8)

23. Money-based political system (10)

26. Basic unit of a living organism (4)

27. Absolute (5)

28. Antiquated (7)

DOWN

1. Removal (10)

2. Large rug (6)

3. Block (4)

4. Changeable (8)

5. Greek letter before kappa (4)

6. Curtain-call cry (5)

8. Pertains (7)

12. Previous (5)

14. Unfriendly (10)

16. Discloses (7)

17. Synonym books (8)

21. Funny people (6)

22. Baby's potential affliction (5)

24. Surefooted wild goat (4)

25. Mosque prayer leader (4)

86

SOLUTION SEE PAGE 268

ACROSS

1. Curses (6)
4. Vast (6)
9. Part of a cowboy boot (4)
10. Profitable (10)
11. Rum cocktail (3,3)
12. Bride's gathering (3,5)
13. Thinks about (9)
15. Fish's breathing organ (4)
16. Police (4)
17. Appraising (9)
21. Exceed a limit (8)
22. Short pleasure trips (6)
24. With thanks (10)
25. Long-tailed reptile (4)
26. Strain (6)
27. Amended (6)

DOWN

1. Choir voice above alto (7)
2. Type of heron (5)
3. Construct again (7)
5. Insult (6)
6. Workings (9)
7. Seaside (7)
8. Scarce (2,5,6)
14. Colon, maybe (9)
16. Larks about; frolics (7)
18. Liked (7)
19. A serve must clear it in tennis (3,4)
20. Crams full (6)
23. Full-length (5)

87

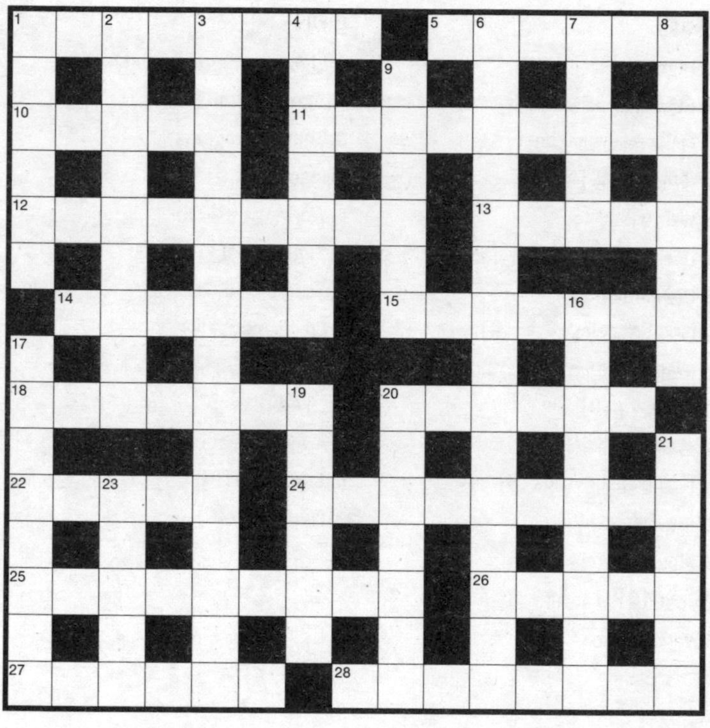

SOLUTION SEE PAGE 269

ACROSS

1. Highly secret (4-4)

5. Business; activity (6)

10. Make mischief (3,2)

11. Annotations (9)

12. Will (9)

13. Decision-making power (3-2)

14. Competitors (6)

15. Cut out (7)

18. Nitpickers (7)

20. District (6)

22. Larceny (5)

24. Faulty (9)

25. Strange events (9)

26. Allium (5)

27. Text format settings (6)

28. Vague notions (8)

DOWN

1. Fireplace floor (6)

2. Sated (9)

3. Desperately wish (4,7,4)

4. Endures (7)

6. Old-time girls' private college (9,6)

7. Fittingly (5)

8. Replies (8)

9. Resembling verse (6)

16. Piece of food (9)

17. Gravestone texts, perhaps (8)

19. Become unhappy (6)

20. Chorus (7)

21. Wimbledon sport (6)

23. The other side (5)

SOLUTION SEE PAGE 269

ACROSS

7. Opinions (5)

8. Engrossed (4)

9. Zero (4)

11. Song words (6)

12. Between day and night (8)

13. Calf-length skirt (4)

15. Workout muscles (3)

16. Key units in any organism (5)

19. Filled, as in a gap (7)

20. Best possible (7)

23. Take by force (5)

25. Maiden (3)

26. Get together (4)

28. Retailer (8)

30. Cause to cover a bigger area (6)

32. Compact by pounding (4)

33. Thorny-stemmed flower (4)

34. Snap (5)

DOWN

1. Large, showy flower (4)

2. Looking forward to (8)

3. Moving at the greatest speed (7)

4. Step (5)

5. Hooked up to the Internet (6)

6. Cross with a looped upper arm (4)

10. Lands (7)

14. Does nothing (5)

17. Depart (5)

18. Practical, not theoretical (7)

21. Childish (8)

22. Excessively conceited person (7)

24. Cooking instructions (6)

27. Hirsute (5)

29. Formal educational test (4)

31. Small notch (4)

89

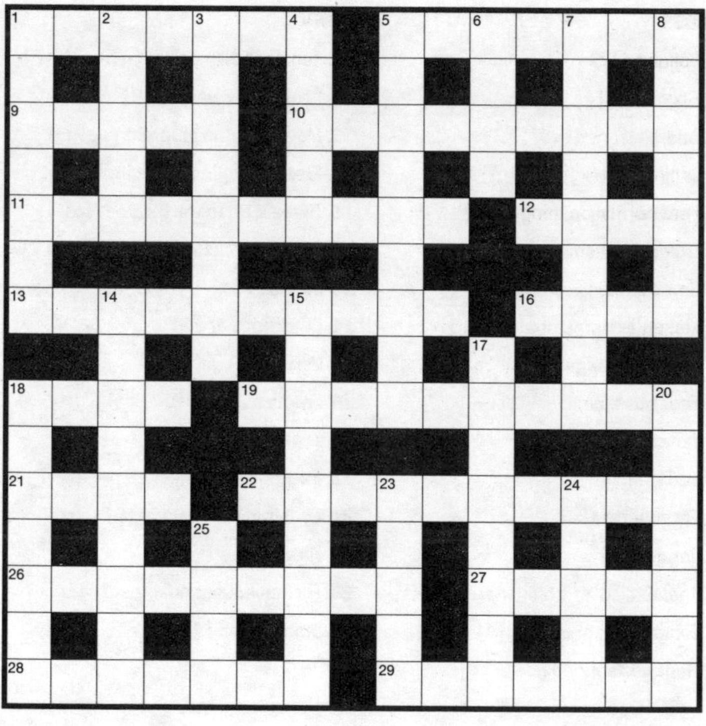

SOLUTION SEE PAGE 270

ACROSS

1. Followed (7)
5. Obedient (7)
9. Adopt as one's own (2-3)
10. Accidental text errors (9)
11. Past normal opening time (5,5)
12. True-north compass (4)
13. Compliance (10)
16. Makes a mistake (4)
18. Plant with edible purple root (4)
19. Those in a vehicle who are not driving (10)
21. Lady's finger plant (4)
22. Be suitable (3,3,4)
26. Tongues (9)
27. Theme (5)
28. Healing treatment (7)
29. Redundant (7)

DOWN

1. Type of keyboard composition (7)
2. Around (5)
3. Relating to writing (8)
4. Disney's flying elephant (5)
5. Diverts attention (9)
6. Go, when playing a game (4)
7. Not emotionally entangled (5-4)
8. Teachings (7)
14. Headroom (9)
15. Astonishingly (9)
17. Creator (8)
18. Pamphlet (7)
20. Opts for (7)
23. Trials (5)
24. Incite; goad (5)
25. Island dance (4)

90

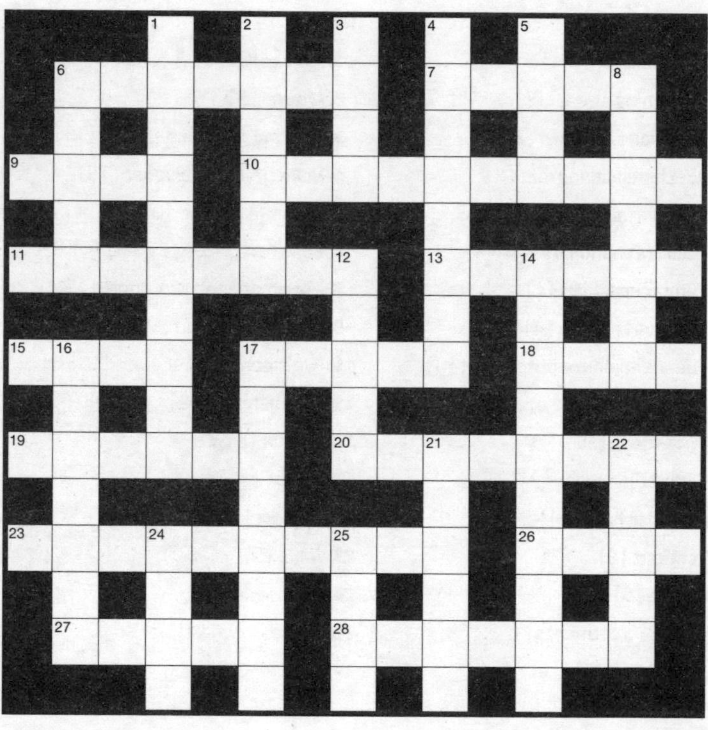

SOLUTION SEE PAGE 270

ACROSS

6. Obstacle (7)
7. Laughing animal (5)
9. Medicine (4)
10. Become active (4,2,4)
11. Singing society (4,4)
13. Close at hand (6)
15. Guitar speakers (4)
17. Hearten (5)
18. Bearing; manner (4)
19. Jail (6)
20. Abandoned (8)
23. Sporadic (10)
26. Slender (4)
27. Upright (5)
28. Practices (7)

DOWN

1. Advances (10)
2. Financial (6)
3. Cut away unwanted parts (4)
4. Bleach (8)
5. Worn to conceal the face (4)
6. Emerald or aquamarine, eg (5)
8. Good-natured (7)
12. Mix together (5)
14. Respect for something (10)
16. Extraordinary, but welcome, event (7)
17. Is made up (8)
21. Water spray (6)
22. Long narrative poems (5)
24. Monkeys (4)
25. Pleasing (4)

91

SOLUTION SEE PAGE 271

ACROSS

1. Bushy, aromatic plant of the mint family (6)
4. Place of worship (6)
9. Pen-stained (4)
10. Written copy (10)
11. Place of business (6)
12. Inclination (8)
13. Suddenly (3,2,4)
15. Adds (4)
16. Keep for later (4)
17. Foes (9)
21. Identity document (8)
22. Sagging (6)
24. Clumsy (10)
25. Selves (4)
26. Smoothed out (6)
27. To the rear, on a ship (6)

DOWN

1. Smattering (7)
2. Tablet pens (5)
3. Out and about (2,3,2)
5. Relaxing (6)
6. Oppress (9)
7. Regards as likely to happen (7)
8. Involvement (13)
14. Prudent (9)
16. A written law (7)
18. Peculiarity (7)
19. Tropical storm (7)
20. Informant (6)
23. Grossly overweight (5)

SOLUTION SEE PAGE 271

ACROSS

9. Drilled-petroleum site (3,4)

10. Reciprocal (7)

11. Transitional period (7)

12. Economizes (7)

13. Cry of dismay (4,5)

15. Fastening (5)

16. Someone who responds to a stimulus (7)

19. Successfully opposes (7)

20. Move back and forth (5)

21. Produced (9)

25. Choices (7)

26. Loud enough to be heard (7)

28. Extract (7)

29. Compete to achieve (7)

DOWN

1. Flowing viscously (6)

2. Very drunk (slang) (6)

3. Equipment (4)

4. Graduates (6)

5. Angry outburst (5,3)

6. Academic's viewpoint? (5,5)

7. More bad-tempered (8)

8. Communications (8)

14. Hide (2,2,6)

16. Makes new again (8)

17. Critical trial step (4,4)

18. Official list of names (8)

22. Subtlety (6)

23. Dining furniture (6)

24. Fears (6)

27. Sand ridge (4)

93

SOLUTION SEE PAGE 272

ACROSS

7. Drip saliva (5)
8. Burn the surface of (4)
9. Leave out (4)
11. Surpass (6)
12. Veils (8)
13. Purpose (4)
15. Four-stringed Hawaiian instrument (3)
16. Incensed (5)
19. Foment (7)
20. Equivalent word (7)
23. Tiny, informally (5)
25. Extended period (3)
26. Buddies (4)
28. Collective (8)
30. Calibrating an instrument (6)
32. At capacity (4)
33. A twist in something straight (4)
34. Massage (5)

DOWN

1. Main point (4)
2. Motion (8)
3. Took away (7)
4. Got up (5)
5. Pillar (6)
6. Gesture without words (4)
10. Modifies (7)
14. Quarrel (5)
17. Relating to a sovereign (5)
18. Ming or Qing (7)
21. Foe (8)
22. Imminent (7)
24. Eat in small bites (6)
27. Adder or asp (5)
29. Set of musical works (4)
31. Undiluted (4)

94

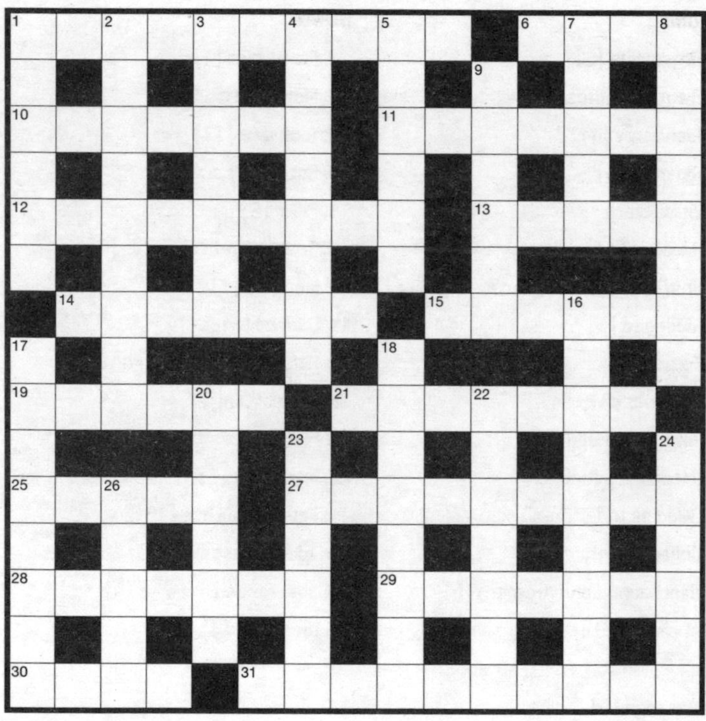

SOLUTION SEE PAGE 272

ACROSS

1. Interprets (10)
6. Feathered creature (4)
10. Conflagration (7)
11. Positions (7)
12. Subsidiary (9)
13. Muslim body covering (5)
14. Initially (7)
15. Judge (6)
19. Historical records (6)
21. Suggest (7)
25. Complain (5)
27. Mediate (9)
28. Vivid pictorial impression (7)
29. With greatest duration (7)
30. Mechanical and repetitive (4)
31. Those that seek to cause fear (10)

DOWN

1. Need for liquid (6)
2. Fondness (9)
3. Leaps quickly (7)
4. Incredibly cute (8)
5. Name formed from a name (6)
7. Most remote from the outside (5)
8. Length between two points (8)
9. Lumberjack's cry (6)
16. Crass (9)
17. Chuckling (8)
18. Someone who waffles (8)
20. Connected (6)
22. Associate (7)
23. Extremely small (6)
24. Extents (6)
26. Scope (5)

95

SOLUTION SEE PAGE 272

ACROSS

6. Family identifier (7)

7. Source of spam? (5)

9. Open-topped tart (4)

10. Someone who can't cope, informally (6,4)

11. Ambulance destination (8)

13. Damage (6)

15. Park boundary ditch (2-2)

17. Split in two (5)

18. Animals used for finding truffles (4)

19. Exertion (6)

20. Moving on hands and knees (8)

23. Tool for adding and removing nails (4,6)

26. Horse's gait (4)

27. Sailing boat (5)

28. Move forward (7)

DOWN

1. Concert keyboard instrument (5,5)

2. Bunny (6)

3. They're used to catch fish (4)

4. Change the meaning of (8)

5. Soft body powder (4)

6. Artillery burst (5)

8. Enduring (7)

12. Small, fragrant shrub (5)

14. Inhabiting (10)

16. Very badly (7)

17. Very short women's shorts (3,5)

21. Reach a destination (6)

22. Snare (5)

24. Candle string (4)

25. Complain; whinge (4)

SOLUTION SEE PAGE 272

ACROSS

1. Most pleasant (6)

4. Plea (6)

9. Thoroughly defeat (4)

10. State of mutual trust and support (10)

11. Bush expedition (6)

12. Wood or iron, eg (4,4)

13. War shout (6,3)

15. Labyrinth (4)

16. Edible freshwater fish (4)

17. Skim a book (5-4)

21. Control column (8)

22. Angers (6)

24. Marginal (10)

25. Aid a crime (4)

26. Many-tiered temple (6)

27. Bikes (6)

DOWN

1. Final Buddhist goal (7)

2. Venomous snake (5)

3. Be enough (7)

5. Juries (6)

6. Recliner (4,5)

7. Spare time (7)

8. Trickery (7-6)

14. Shoving (9)

16. Very near (5,2)

18. In the same way (7)

19. Hunter's wall trophy (7)

20. Was audibly wistful (6)

23. Insignificant (5)

97

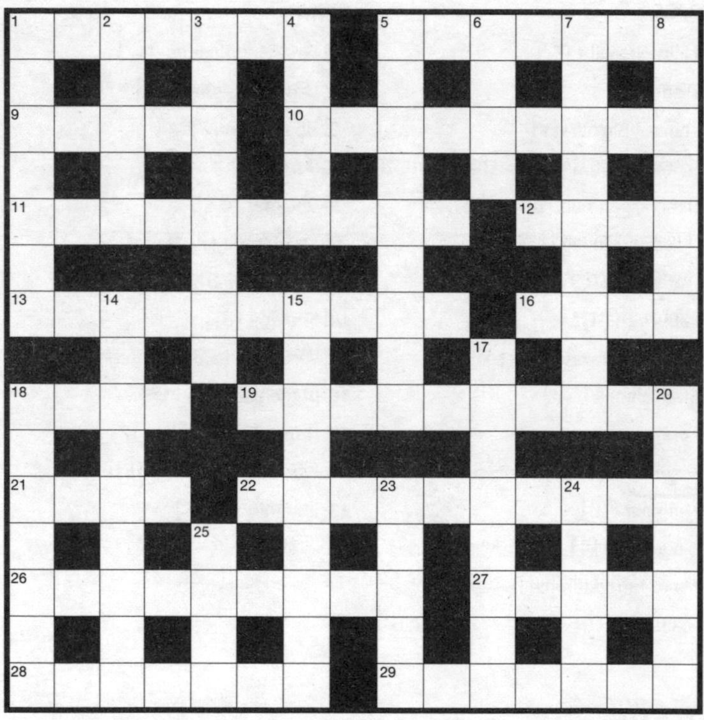

SOLUTION SEE PAGE 274

ACROSS

1. Still in progress (7)

5. Onward (7)

9. Special reward (5)

10. Done through free will (9)

11. Needed for admission? (10)

12. Floating ice field (4)

13. In error (10)

16. Tidal outflows (4)

18. Prolonged medical sleep (4)

19. Remote countryside (10)

21. Settee (4)

22. Features (10)

26. Held back (9)

27. Hindu forehead decoration (5)

28. General health and fortunes (7)

29. Tofu base (7)

DOWN

1. Best (7)

2. Shine brightly (5)

3. As good as certain (2,3,3)

4. Donates (5)

5. Achieved (9)

6. Tirade (4)

7. Accessible (9)

8. Lack of moisture (7)

14. Event before the last round (9)

15. Being (9)

17. Very likely (8)

18. Moneymaking investment (4,3)

20. Period (7)

23. Travels on (5)

24. On edge (5)

25. Heroic tale (4)

SOLUTION SEE PAGE 274

ACROSS

7. Stipulations (5)

8. At what time? (4)

9. Slippery; slick (4)

11. Entirely (6)

12. Depth measurement (8)

13. Earthquake points of origin (4)

15. Elongated fish (3)

16. Take as one's own (5)

19. Ruined; spoiled (7)

20. Skyline (7)

23. Mails (5)

25. Zero (3)

26. Speedy (4)

28. Tubular pasta (8)

30. Try hard (6)

32. Adult male deer (4)

33. Tended to the weeds, maybe (4)

34. Ceases (5)

DOWN

1. 'I suppose so' (4)

2. Insinuating (8)

3. Simple wind instrument (7)

4. Enter (5)

5. Phrased (6)

6. Design (4)

10. Laid out, as a book (7)

14. Egg-shaped (5)

17. Schemes (5)

18. Atheistic (7)

21. Relaxed (8)

22. Someone with internal knowledge (7)

24. Sketches (6)

27. Soft, sheepskin leather (5)

29. Sad to say (4)

31. Ballot selection (4)

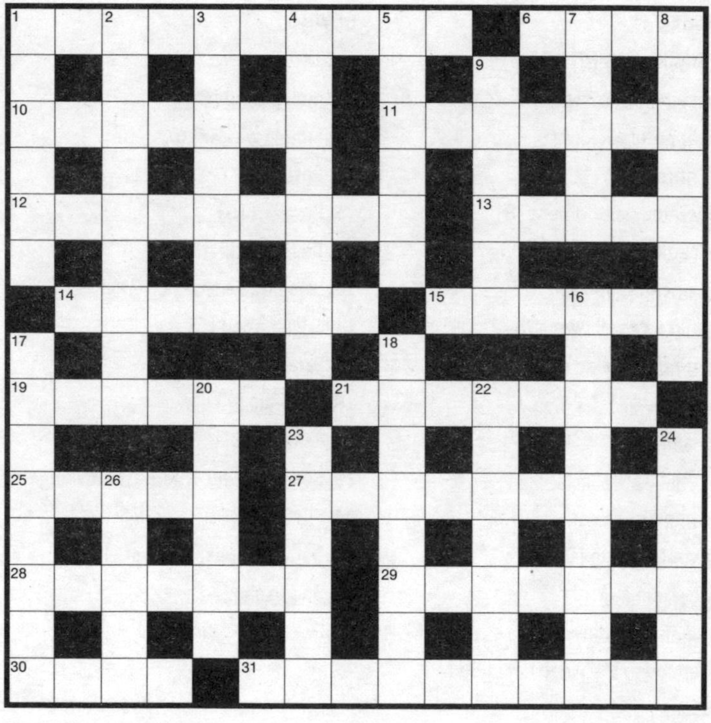

SOLUTION SEE PAGE 275

ACROSS

1. Favoured (10)

6. Celestial Christmas vision (4)

10. Rotate (7)

11. Order (7)

12. Allows (9)

13. Lawful (5)

14. Joking (7)

15. Dash (6)

19. Octave (6)

21. Like many magazines (7)

25. "Halo" fan? (5)

27. Cooked plainly (2,7)

28. Orchestral drum set (7)

29. Bans (7)

30. Top of a bottle (4)

31. Atomic scientists, eg (10)

DOWN

1. Equality (6)

2. Entailing (9)

3. Badly brought up (3-4)

4. Choosing (8)

5. Abundance (6)

7. Pluck a guitar string (5)

8. Fragrant (8)

9. Hire (6)

16. Extremely funny (9)

17. Become more intense (8)

18. Joins (8)

20. Possibility of danger (6)

22. Of very great size (7)

23. Uncouth (6)

24. Explosions (6)

26. Ape (5)

100

SOLUTION SEE PAGE 275

ACROSS

6. Adding up (7)

7. Hawaiian greeting (5)

9. Polynesian shrub used for narcotics (4)

10. Deter (10)

11. Allocated (8)

13. Foreign nanny (2,4)

15. Small songbird (4)

17. Inspire (5)

18. Ibuprofen target (4)

19. Swear to (6)

20. Causes to happen (8)

23. Biased information (10)

26. Globes (4)

27. Ballroom dance (5)

28. Opposed (7)

DOWN

1. Irascibility (10)

2. Obscured (6)

3. Eras (4)

4. Deliberate damage (8)

5. Tart (4)

6. Makes watertight (5)

8. Heartache (7)

12. Deduction of money (5)

14. Recreation area (10)

16. Comes back (7)

17. Essential; fundamental (8)

21. Kind of (2,1,3)

22. Automaton (5)

24. Long, slender piece of wood or metal (4)

25. At hand (4)

SOLUTION SEE PAGE 276

ACROSS

1. Gave the impression of being (6)

4. Not familiar (6)

9. Appendage (4)

10. Camera image (10)

11. Artist's room (6)

12. Gifted (8)

13. Game point, in tennis (9)

15. Low, marshy lands (4)

16. Prolonged hostility (4)

17. Tolerant (9)

21. Duration of a person's existence (8)

22. Change into (6)

24. Oversees (10)

25. British 'Count' (4)

26. Proceeds to a room, perhaps (6)

27. Of hidden meaning (6)

DOWN

1. Moved (7)

2. Receded (5)

3. Bold or daring feat (7)

5. Spaghetti-like strip of pasta (6)

6. Rigorous (9)

7. Push, as in a button (7)

8. Soft and lumpy dairy product (7,6)

14. Diversion (9)

16. Lack of success (7)

18. Mission (7)

19. Consisting of numbers (7)

20. Second-place medal (6)

23. Large, strong box (5)

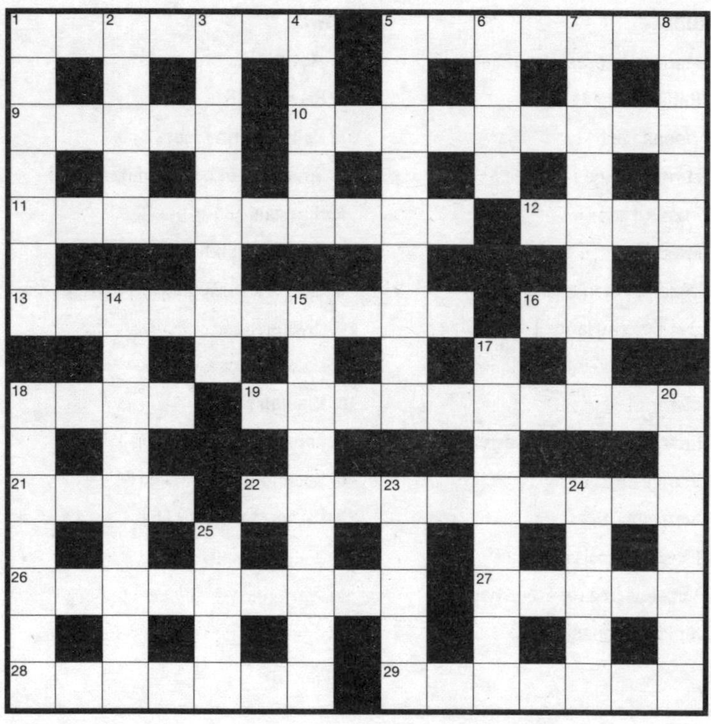

SOLUTION SEE PAGE 276

ACROSS

1. Monetary resources (7)
5. Public transport (7)
9. Weeps (5)
10. Confront (9)
11. Expert (10)
12. Feverish fit (4)
13. Diplomatic official (10)
16. Ova (4)
18. Extremely serious or urgent (4)
19. Young person (10)
21. Grow faint and disappear (4)
22. Device circulating fresh air (10)
26. Shortens (9)
27. Figure of speech (5)
28. Took out to dinner, eg (7)
29. Makes sorrowful (7)

DOWN

1. Pendulous ornamental shrub (7)
2. Overly trusting (5)
3. Most vile (8)
4. Perform exceptionally well (5)
5. Fungal fruiting body (9)
6. Permitted (4)
7. Jewish house of worship (9)
8. Sways back and forth (7)
14. Ceilidh, eg (4,5)
15. Spoke to (9)
17. Remote (8)
18. Shortfall (7)
20. Goals (7)
23. Jobs (5)
24. Particular cut of loin steak (1-4)
25. Exploit (4)

103

SOLUTION SEE PAGE 177

ACROSS

7. Large, imposing residence on an estate (5)
8. Poke or jab (4)
9. Summit (4)
11. In a dormant state (6)
12. Seeming (8)
13. Nasty cut (4)
15. Refusal, slangily (3)
16. Slacker (5)
19. Provide with healthy food (7)
20. Social group (7)
23. Conclude (5)
25. Hawaiian floral garland (3)
26. Suffers as a result of something (4)
28. Took manual control of, as a machine (8)
30. Dwells (6)
32. Water surrounded by land (4)
33. Journeyed by horse (4)
34. Memento (5)

DOWN

1. Lowest vocal range (4)
2. At the same time (8)
3. Respire (7)
4. Modify (5)
5. Consecrated (6)
6. Faculty head (4)
10. Suitability (7)
14. Nut from an oak tree (5)
17. The act of coming in (5)
18. Of current relevance (7)
21. Confine (8)
22. By the time mentioned (7)
24. Gained (6)
27. Anxiety (5)
29. Calf meat (4)
31. Barnyard bleaters (4)

104

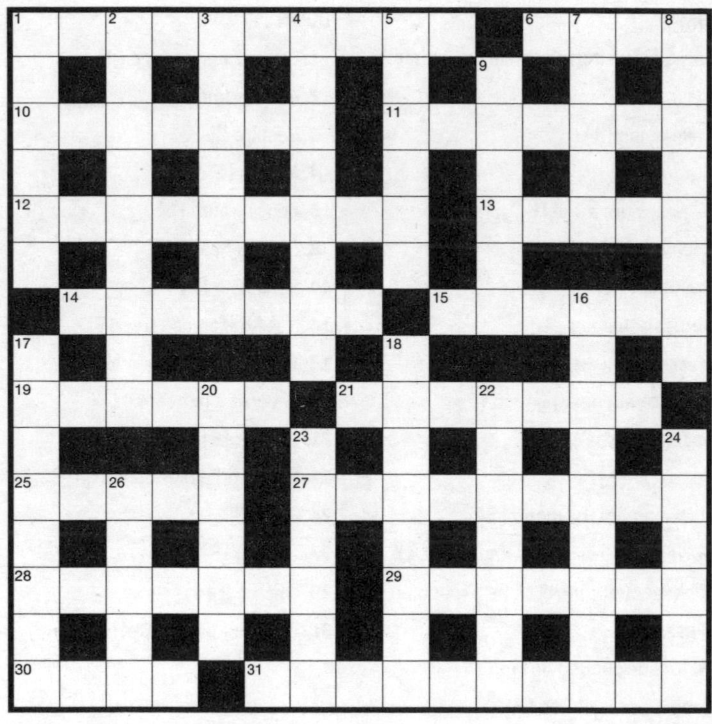

SOLUTION SEE PAGE 277

ACROSS

1. Efficient in terms of expense (10)

6. Swindle (4)

10. Frame of reference (7)

11. Adversaries (7)

12. Those who owe government tithes (9)

13. Shadow during an eclipse (5)

14. Not adhere to a plan (2,5)

15. On land, not sea (6)

19. Naval standard (6)

21. Calculate (7)

25. Raw vegetable dish (5)

27. Terrific (9)

28. Underlying stone (7)

29. Block of frozen water (3,4)

30. Philosophical male principle (4)

31. Tackles (10)

DOWN

1. Fire up (6)

2. Offensive (9)

3. Outside; unenclosed (4,3)

4. Ultimately (2,3,3)

5. Someone discriminating by seniority (6)

7. Ascend (5)

8. Errors (8)

9. Concert sites (6)

16. Hapless (3,2,4)

17. With due prudence (8)

18. Happen at the same time (8)

20. Male child sponsored at a baptism (6)

22. Current (7)

23. Become active (6)

24. Foreigners (6)

26. Burdened (5)

105

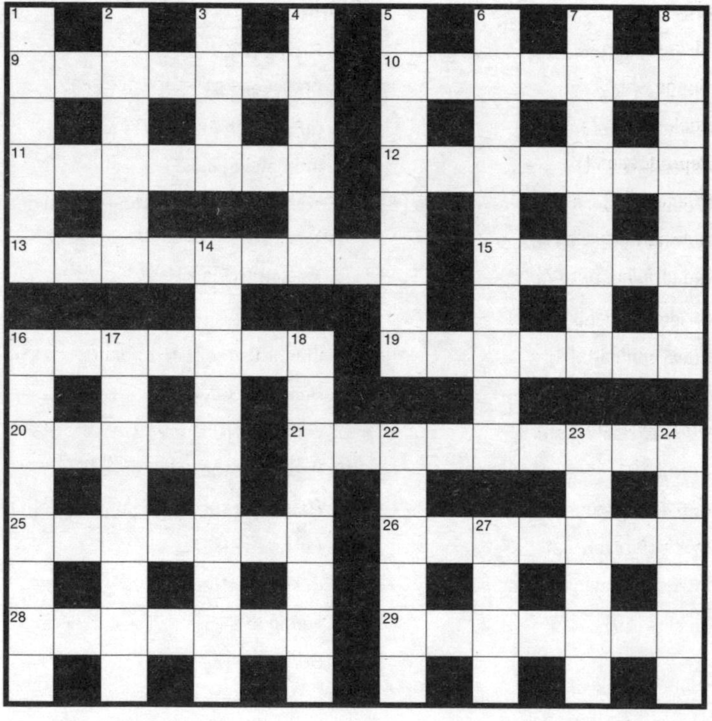

SOLUTION SEE PAGE 278

ACROSS

9. Melancholy (7)
10. On the way (2,5)
11. Adolescent (7)
12. Reproduction (7)
13. Practical (9)
15. Rule as monarch (5)
16. Small, juicy fruit (7)
19. Accomplished (7)
20. Church tenets (5)
21. Hugely (9)
25. Greatly frighten (7)
26. Fuss (7)
28. Generally (7)
29. Dressed (7)

DOWN

1. In a state of disrepair (4-2)
2. Former Spanish currency (6)
3. Self-important person (4)
4. Agree to (6)
5. Withdraws (8)
6. Ratio (10)
7. Of a court of law (8)
8. Stayed (8)
14. Involving machinery (10)
16. Summation (8)
17. Seen (8)
18. Toddler's pedal vehicle (8)
22. Reciprocal (6)
23. Get on board (6)
24. Gives way (6)
27. Type of grain (4)

106

SOLUTION SEE PAGE 278

ACROSS

1. Not confident (8)
5. Insist upon (6)
10. Quickly lowers the head (5)
11. Answers (9)
12. Chivalrous guy (9)
13. Rhinal (5)
14. Prejudices (6)
15. Inexpensively (7)
18. Entirely natural (7)
20. Within a train (6)
22. Rugged (5)
24. Correction (9)
25. Wistful thoughts (9)
26. No longer a child (5)
27. Lampoon (6)
28. Disclosed (8)

DOWN

1. Blue shade (6)
2. Endorsing (9)
3. Daydreams (7,2,3,3)
4. Continues (7)
6. Friendly understanding between factions (7,8)
7. Nuclei and electrons (5)
8. Demonstrates (8)
9. Hospital department (6)
16. Everlasting (9)
17. That which is inside (8)
19. Edit (6)
20. Overhead projector sheet (7)
21. Declared (6)
23. Not yet hardened (5)

107

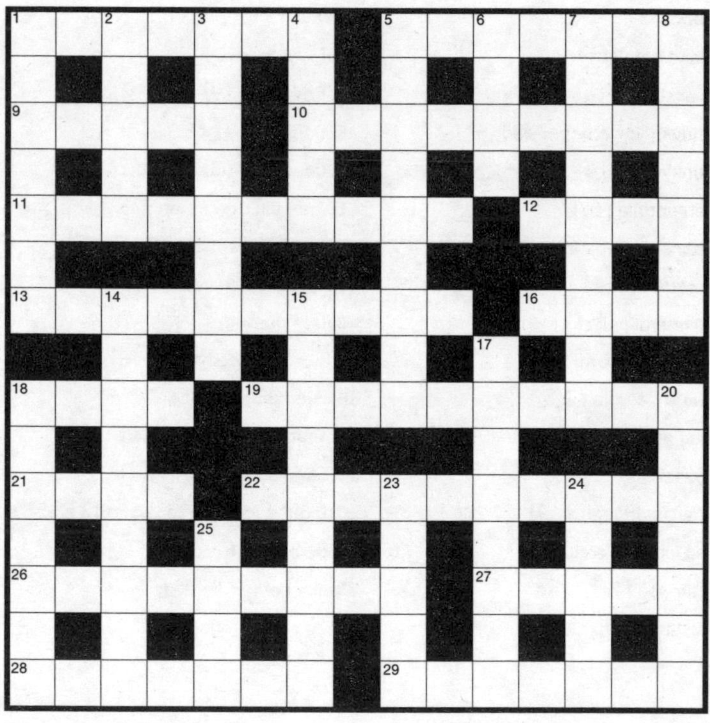

SOLUTION SEE PAGE 279

ACROSS

1. Made irate (7)

5. Those hooked on something (7)

9. Showing no emotion (5)

10. Book rooms (9)

11. Perceptibly (10)

12. Former Italian currency unit (4)

13. Communicate by letter (10)

16. Collateral property (4)

18. Sharp punch, informally (4)

19. Royal Navy sailor rank (4,6)

21. Ride a wave (4)

22. Fallacious (10)

26. Possession (9)

27. Static (5)

28. Orator (7)

29. Clothed (7)

DOWN

1. Popular poison, in literature (7)

2. Leave somewhere (2,3)

3. Used again (8)

4. Fourth Greek letter (5)

5. Emergency transport vehicle (9)

6. Small shot of spirits (4)

7. Disapproval (9)

8. Bear the weight of (7)

14. Allusion (9)

15. Book producer (9)

17. Family member (8)

18. Diagonally moving pieces (7)

20. Logically inverted (7)

23. Fatty compound (5)

24. Concepts (5)

25. Long walk (4)

SOLUTION SEE PAGE 279

ACROSS

1. Tried to catch cod, eg (6)

4. Hang loosely (6)

9. Facts (4)

10. Synchronize (10)

11. Feeling of sickness (6)

12. Software training lesson (8)

13. Someone who brings a legal action (9)

15. 'Stop, Rover!' (4)

16. Gap (4)

17. Gaining entry to (9)

21. Work in a linked way (8)

22. Money earned (6)

24. For general use (3-7)

25. Website visitor (4)

26. Wanders (6)

27. Not these (6)

DOWN

1. Post sent to celebrities (3,4)

2. Goes to the mall, perhaps (5)

3. Bewitch (7)

5. Financial checks (6)

6. Produces (9)

7. Tidal river mouth (7)

8. Reinforcement (13)

14. Irritability (3,6)

16. Manages (7)

18. Distinguished (7)

19. Figures (7)

20. Justly (6)

23. Reason (5)

109

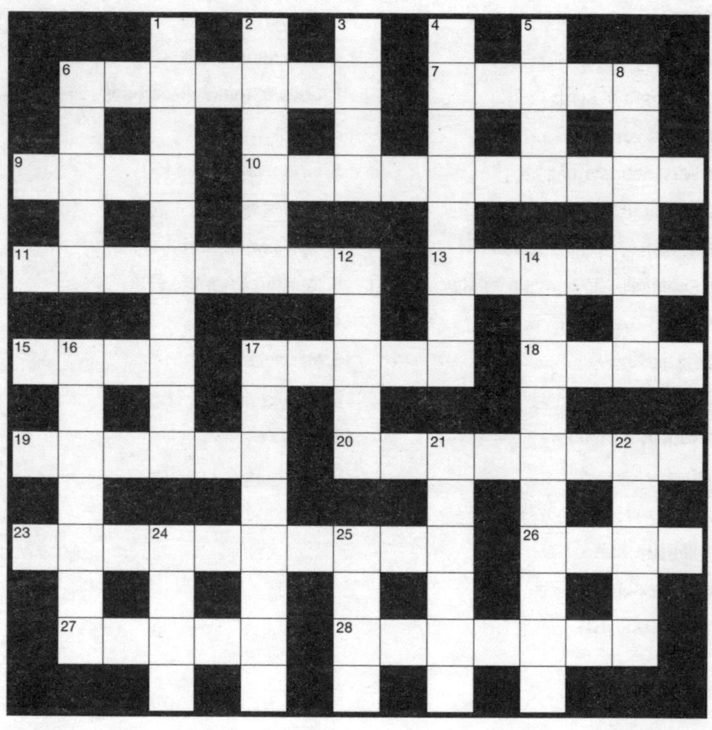

SOLUTION SEE PAGE 280

ACROSS

6. Unvarying (7)

7. Strength of spirit? (5)

9. A story of heroic adventure (4)

10. Was inconsistent (10)

11. Cut short (5,3)

13. Internal (6)

15. Stalk (4)

17. At the side of (5)

18. Explosive munition (4)

19. Rarely encountered (6)

20. Most out of practice (8)

23. Dining venue (10)

26. Implement that's used to smooth clothes (4)

27. Reconnaissance soldier (5)

28. Brings into a country (7)

DOWN

1. Statement denying responsibility (10)

2. Blanket wrap (6)

3. 'I agree!' (4)

4. Orthography (8)

5. Twisted-metal neckband (4)

6. Stimulant drug, in slang (5)

8. Liberty (7)

12. Surface for walking on (5)

14. Ancillary (10)

16. Entry documents (7)

17. Sufficient (8)

21. Workout exercises (3-3)

22. Casino machines (5)

24. System of weights for precious metals (4)

25. Having a keen desire (4)

110

SOLUTION SEE PAGE 280

ACROSS

7. You, eg (5)

8. One who acts upon something (4)

9. Stupid person (4)

11. Useless (6)

12. Room heater (8)

13. Graceful, white waterbird (4)

15. Police officer (3)

16. Savoury meat-stock jelly (5)

19. Supersede (7)

20. Use again (7)

23. Sacred song (5)

25. Santa's helper? (3)

26. Poultry pen (4)

28. With dignity, musically (8)

30. Gesture (6)

32. Unarmed combat sport (4)

33. Bloke (4)

34. Declare invalid (5)

DOWN

1. Ballerina's skirt (4)

2. Across the country (8)

3. Open to bribes, perhaps (7)

4. Commerce (5)

5. Principles (6)

6. Vocal range (4)

10. Show-off (7)

14. Days and days (5)

17. Inuit house (5)

18. Fragrance (7)

21. Boating (8)

22. Separation (7)

24. Teaching unit (6)

27. Attest (5)

29. Water (4)

31. Obligation (4)

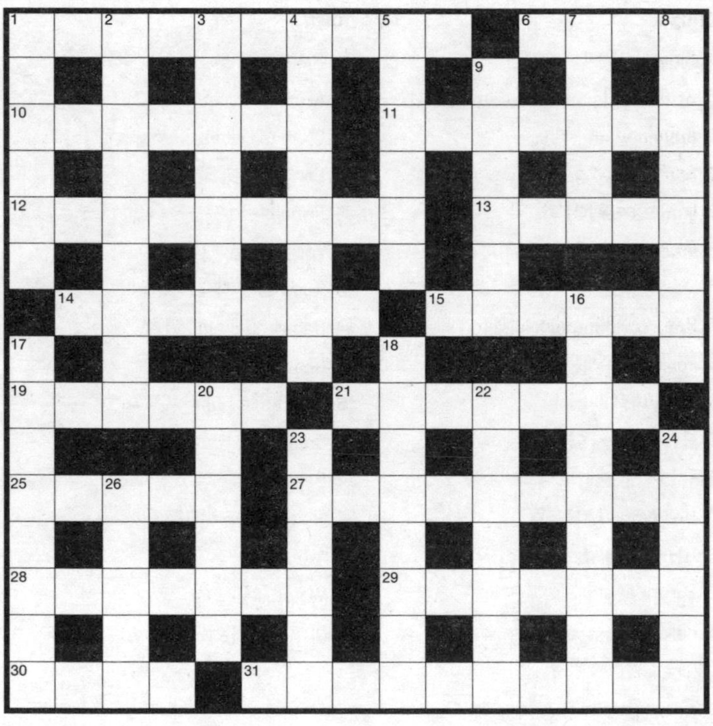

SOLUTION SEE PAGE 281

ACROSS

1. Finale (10)
6. Swami (4)
10. Appalling act (7)
11. Apprehending; catching (7)
12. Oversensitive (9)
13. Frenzy (5)
14. Violins (7)
15. Regard with respect (6)
19. Fourscore (6)
21. Faithfulness (7)
25. Music artist's compilation (5)
27. Throat lozenge (5,4)
28. Higher in value (7)
29. Noms de plume (7)
30. Be uncritically fond of (4)
31. Publicizes (10)

DOWN

1. Large groups of people (6)
2. Informing (9)
3. Erudite (7)
4. Example (8)
5. Sixteenths of a pound (6)
7. Association of workers (5)
8. Installs newer software (8)
9. Recorded a video (6)
16. Hobbies (9)
17. Mad (8)
18. Inhabitants (8)
20. Entices (6)
22. Someone with no religious faith (7)
23. Afraid (6)
24. Muscle tics (6)
26. Sound made by a sheep or goat (5)

112

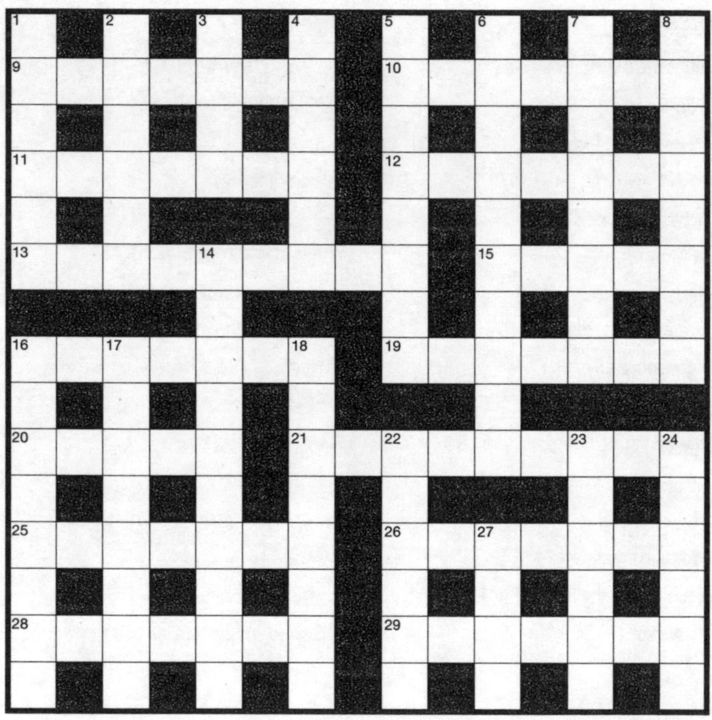

SOLUTION SEE PAGE 281

ACROSS

9. Become aware of again (7)

10. Supply (7)

11. Using every effort (4,3)

12. Withdraw (7)

13. Driver's unseen region (5,4)

15. Pivotal (5)

16. Reaches a destination (7)

19. Meet (7)

20. Overall amount (5)

21. Take turns (9)

25. Fell (7)

26. Outcomes (7)

28. Coach (7)

29. Non-professional (7)

DOWN

1. Modular house (6)

2. It neutralizes an acid (6)

3. Saint's aura (4)

4. Together (2,4)

5. Performs surgery (8)

6. Mail boss (10)

7. Essential dietary compounds (8)

8. In your mind (8)

14. Evolving (10)

16. Remedy (8)

17. Reasoned (8)

18. Criterion (8)

22. Yarn (6)

23. Coalition forces (6)

24. Guarantee (6)

27. Hit sharply, as an insect (4)

113

SOLUTION SEE PAGE 282

ACROSS

1. Inhaler target (6)
4. Chatty (6)
9. Dipped in yolk (4)
10. Music from a movie (10)
11. Walk softly (6)
12. Cordially (8)
13. Capricious (9)
15. Masterfully (4)
16. Small restaurant (4)
17. Free (2,7)
21. Computer file, perhaps (8)
22. Deems (6)
24. Transition (10)
25. Prison sentence (4)
26. Perspires (6)
27. Hindu retreat (6)

DOWN

1. Madder (7)
2. Lovers' meet-up (5)
3. Get the wrong idea, perhaps (7)
5. Extreme experience (6)
6. Easily annoyed (9)
7. In the vicinity (7)
8. Definitive (13)
14. Sway (9)
16. Togs (7)
18. Wounds (7)
19. Algebraic rule (7)
20. Up to date (6)
23. Discourage (5)

114

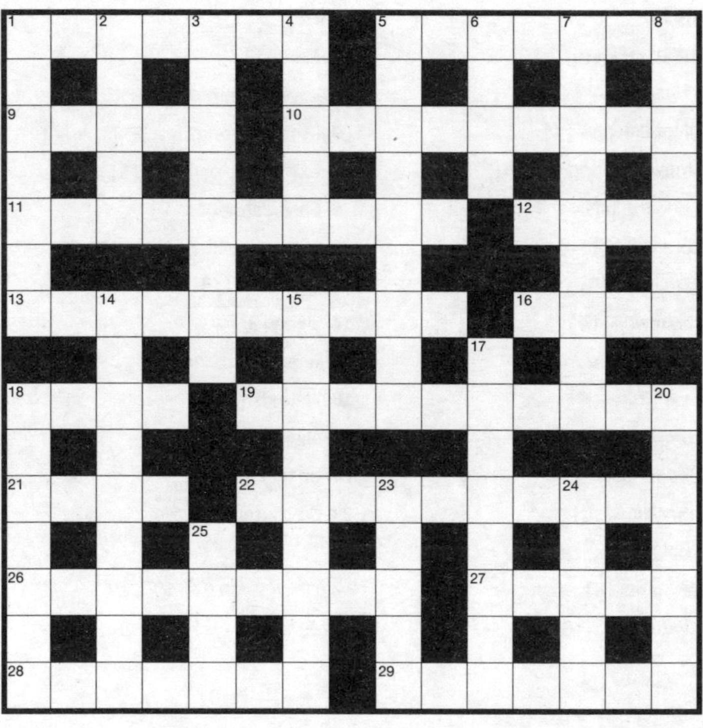

SOLUTION SEE PAGE 282

ACROSS

1. Wins a victory over (7)

5. Hazy (7)

9. More mentally fit (5)

10. Vowel's counterpart (9)

11. Place of higher education (10)

12. Ancient Roman garment (4)

13. Locked up (6,4)

16. Produces an egg (4)

18. Remedy (4)

19. Female partner (10)

21. Crooked (4)

22. Benefits (10)

26. Allegiance (9)

27. Extent (5)

28. Appears (7)

29. Digression (7)

DOWN

1. Bother (7)

2. Truffles, eg (5)

3. Consenting (8)

4. Bags (5)

5. Abnormal (9)

6. Very short hairstyle (4)

7. Ornate (9)

8. Formalized ceremonies (7)

14. Equine footwear (9)

15. Roofed and walled structures (9)

17. Brothers (8)

18. Waterfall (7)

20. Sweet course (7)

23. Proficient (5)

24. He lives in a lamp (5)

25. Rugged cliff or rock face (4)

SOLUTION SEE PAGE 283

ACROSS

7. Transform (5)
8. Champion (4)
9. Line about which a body rotates (4)
11. Ordained people (6)
12. Drinks (8)
13. Mother (4)
15. Drag with great effort (3)
16. Donkeys (5)
19. Duke's wife (7)
20. Three-part work (7)
23. Musical speed (5)
25. Not bright (3)
26. Bundles of money (4)
28. Least expensive (8)
30. Loud, shrill cry (6)
32. Travel on (4)
33. Come to an end (4)
34. Not suitable (5)

DOWN

1. Monk's hood (4)
2. Draw near (8)
3. Letter; dispatch (7)
4. Spoken (5)
5. Spoons for serving liquids (6)
6. What can be seen right now (4)
10. Mascara target (7)
14. Pointed, as an angle (5)
17. Inched (5)
18. Pledge (7)
21. Decreasing (8)
22. Release (7)
24. Toyed (6)
27. Touch or taste, eg (5)
29. Wig material (4)
31. Lemon juice, eg (4)

116

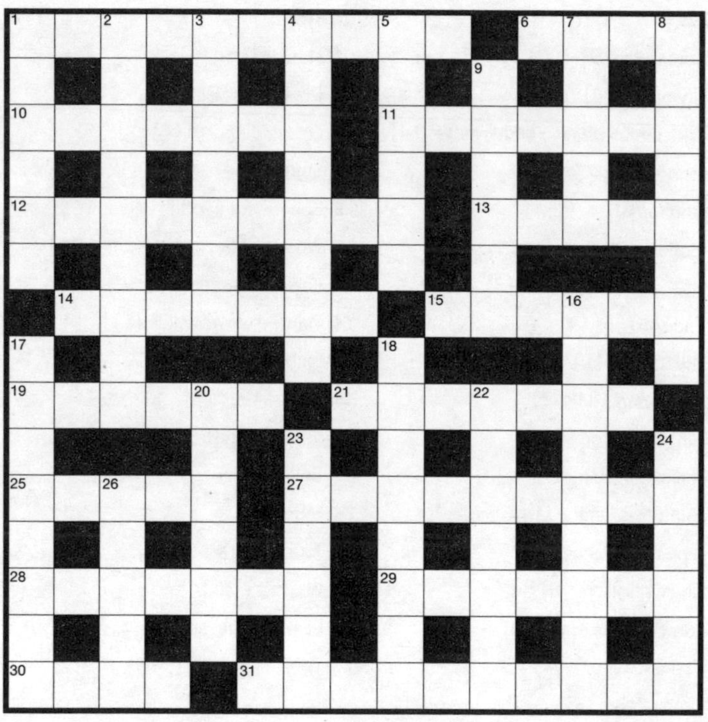

SOLUTION SEE PAGE 283

ACROSS

1. Not practical (10)
6. Volcanic product (4)
10. Dark green, leafy vegetable (7)
11. Cutting slightly (7)
12. Stand for (9)
13. Bamboo-eating animal (5)
14. Pulverized (7)
15. Handy (6)
19. In truth; absolutely (6)
21. Taking shape (7)
25. Male duck (5)
27. Possible pawn move in chess (2,7)
28. Caught fire (7)
29. Surprise (7)
30. Men (4)
31. Secondary results (2-8)

DOWN

1. Hesitant (6)
2. Spoken quietly (9)
3. Newspaper purchasers (7)
4. Accomplishes (8)
5. Extent (6)
7. Straighten up (5)
8. It can be said that (8)
9. Targeting views (6)
16. Amazing (9)
17. Manipulating, as in financial records (8)
18. Songwriter (8)
20. Chooses (6)
22. Hot-tasting yellow condiment (7)
23. Lethal (6)
24. Drives (6)
26. Harass (5)

117

SOLUTION SEE PAGE 284

ACROSS

6. Subside (3,4)

7. Parody (5)

9. Naked (4)

10. Defying authority (10)

11. Felon (8)

13. Causing great distress (6)

15. Raced (4)

17. Beneficiaries of a will (5)

18. Tree associated with tropical climes (4)

19. Let (6)

20. Sets up (8)

23. Marry (slang) (3,7)

26. Leave a room (4)

27. Neck warmer (5)

28. Pelting (7)

DOWN

1. Electoral vote on an issue (10)

2. Beastly (6)

3. Someone who looks down on others (4)

4. Separates (8)

5. Indian flatbread (4)

6. One of Snow White's helpers (5)

8. Of a river (7)

12. Healing-hands therapy (5)

14. Sorted like a dictionary (10)

16. Tends to choose (7)

17. Get on (3,2,3)

21. Salt component (6)

22. Fibbing (5)

24. Warmth (4)

25. Pelvic projections (4)

118

SOLUTION SEE PAGE 284

ACROSS

1. Implants (6)

4. Opposite of alkaline (6)

9. Good fortune (4)

10. Most important things (10)

11. Multi-speaker sound (6)

12. Guiltless (8)

13. Finishes university (9)

15. Crafty (4)

16. Specified amount of medicine (4)

17. Merge together into a group (9)

21. Pin to the floor (4,4)

22. Pre-Christmas period (6)

24. Merging (10)

25. Karaoke for two? (4)

26. Spoke (6)

27. Imbeciles (6)

DOWN

1. Earth's midriff? (7)

2. Bread maker (5)

3. Educational award (7)

5. Considerate (6)

6. Separating (9)

7. Without pollution (7)

8. Road designer (5,8)

14. Small whirlwind (4,5)

16. Leave prematurely (4,3)

18. Responded (7)

19. Passageways (7)

20. Unrefined (6)

23. Make a visual recording (5)

119

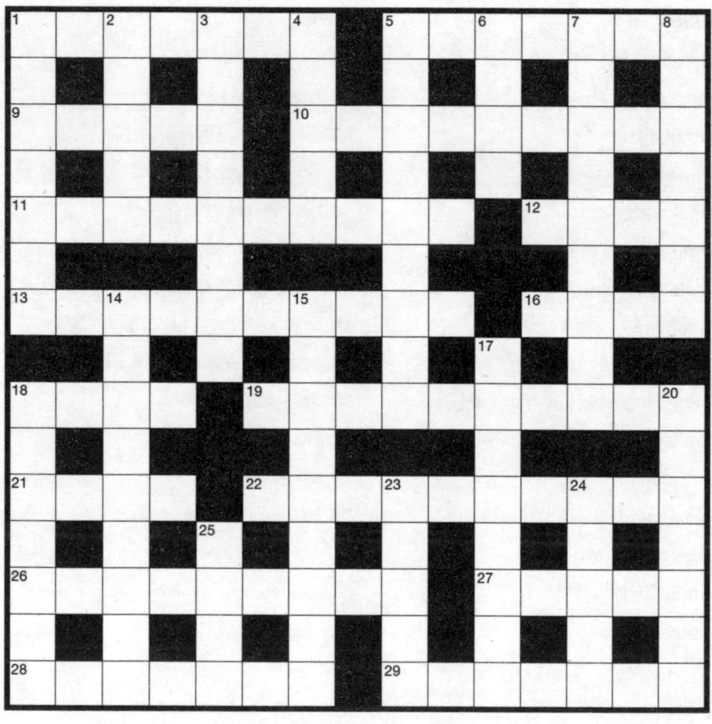

SOLUTION SEE PAGE 285

ACROSS

1. Moreover (7)
5. Forbidden by law (7)
9. Unfolds (5)
10. Adult males (9)
11. Proponents (10)
12. Petty quarrel (4)
13. Marking with a sharp object (10)
16. Tough and lean (4)
18. Go against (4)
19. Points in the right direction (10)
21. Sea-based armed service (4)
22. Bad luck (10)
26. Evacuation siren (4,5)
27. Identifying piece of paper (5)
28. Immature frog (7)
29. Wanted (7)

DOWN

1. Uses Chrome or Safari, perhaps (7)
2. Slumber (5)
3. Twists out of shape (8)
4. The ability to see (5)
5. Absence of education (9)
6. Idle in a relaxed way (4)
7. Chance to get ahead, in tennis? (4,5)
8. Verbose (7)
14. Got well again (9)
15. Violent windstorm (9)
17. Surprises (8)
18. Advantage (7)
20. Gave the letters that make up a word (7)
23. Well-known (5)
24. Dark-brown pigment (5)
25. Sandwich dressing (4)

SOLUTION SEE PAGE 285

ACROSS

7. March (5)

8. Feral (4)

9. Beats on a serve (4)

11. GPS direction options (6)

12. Offered marriage (8)

13. European currency (4)

15. Utilize (3)

16. Consumed (5)

19. Sticks (7)

20. Chaos (7)

23. Rubbish (5)

25. Flightless bird (3)

26. Categorize (4)

28. It might be thrown at a wedding (8)

30. Soil (6)

32. Welt (4)

33. Sneak a look (4)

34. Employing (5)

DOWN

1. Therefore (4)

2. Adjourn (8)

3. Less complex (7)

4. Colloquialism (5)

5. Triangular Indian snack (6)

6. 'Look this way!' (4)

10. Takes for granted (7)

14. Beneath (5)

17. The clear sky (5)

18. Pander (7)

21. Reply (8)

22. Updated (7)

24. Without risk (6)

27. Dance moves (5)

29. Cows or bulls (4)

31. Taboo act (2-2)

SOLUTIONS

1

UNCERTAINTY
O O O D O
EVENLY YOGI
I S L
SCOPE CLOCK
E R I R
ASHES ACTED
P B V
COLA RETAIL
V R A O C
PARENTHESES

2

ECONOMIES
P U O E N
RENDS ALDER
O N E N E
PRIM FIESTA
O N B E I C
SIGNED SMUT
A H T I I
LARVA HELLO
H L U A N
CONFIGURE

SOLUTIONS

3

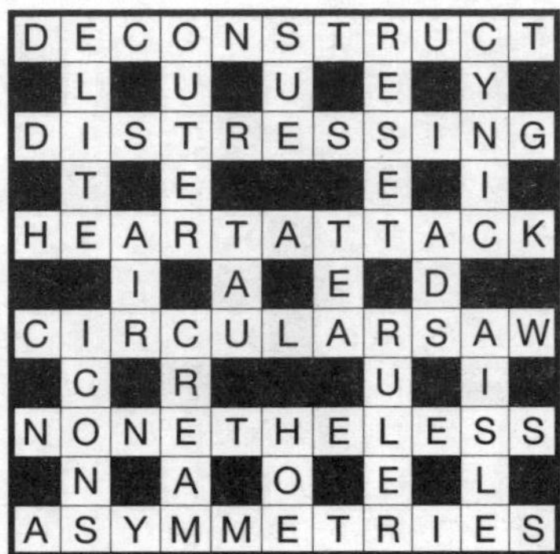
DECONSTRUCT
L U U E Y
DISTRESSING
T E E I
HEARTATTACK
I A E D
CIRCULARSAW
C R U I
NONETHELESS
N A O E L
ASYMMETRIES

4

TRANSFORMED
E O I A I
WAFT BUTTIN
L H S T G
VISIT EVERY
Z N I E
WEIGH STATE
I D M A A
DRYICE MAIL
T L N I N
HELPFULNESS

5

AUTOMATING
N R I N O
GLOBAL SOBS
E S P
CAMPS FINDS
S E R I
THORN NEIGH
F D I
AMMO ROBOTS
O R A Y A
ADMITTEDLY

6

R E FUNNY
CONMOTO A O
T P RIVER
MACES M E E
T R GAS
BELOW LEASH
RAT V P
C F S CEDED
HEART R E
E I ENHANCE
WIRED L H

SOLUTIONS

7

CRAFTSWOMAN
A L E B R
MISUSE SAME
S S C
FIRST QUICK
N H R O
AGLOW GENRE
R F R
SPIT LOCKED
I E E A C
APPROXIMATE

8

ASSASSINATE
W I C B A
FAIRER BARS
L M E S E
ULNA WASHED
O I M X
DWELLS OOPS
E X M O E
BUTS ACTING
U R R H S
GRANDMASTER

9

ADJUDICATED
V O R D M
ACKACK DOUR
I E S R L
LURKS DECAY
N N S T
ODDER ASHEN
E A G Y E
GRID HOPPER
G E E E V
GOLDRESERVE

10

UNHEALTHY
T E N E A P
EVENT SUPER
L I S P O
EMBERS ZINC
S R E S E E
CLAD SPARES
O V S O S
PIANO KENDO
E D A E U R
COMPONENT

SOLUTIONS

13

DEDICATING
U R O N O
SMARMY SPOT
T W P A E
SUBJECT PAD
T A T O E I
ORC EMBARGO
R K A B U
MOSS SCRAPS
D I C C L
DISCJOCKEY

14

TERMINOLOGY
M E E U U
SPAM STATIC
O B T D C
SWEEP STOMA
E R O E
GROSS SUNNY
R C B C T
ARCANE HAIL
S U A E O
SURROUNDING

15

16

SOLUTIONS

17

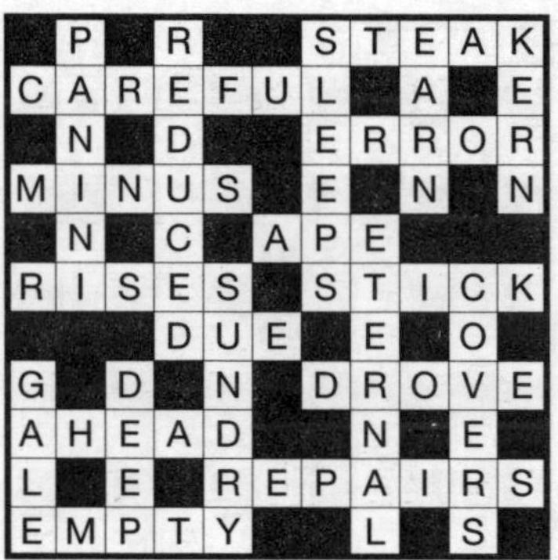
P R STEAK
CAREFUL A E
N D ERROR
MINUS E N N
N C APE
RISES STICK
DUE E O
G D N DROVE
AHEAD N E
L E REPAIRS
EMPTY L S

18

THERAPEUTIC
R A L N O O
ATTEMPT RUN
N S O T C
SIPS IMMUNE
P H S B R N
ORALLY NEXT
R N O F R
TAT GORILLA
E O A E E T
DEMONSTRATE

19

20

21

22

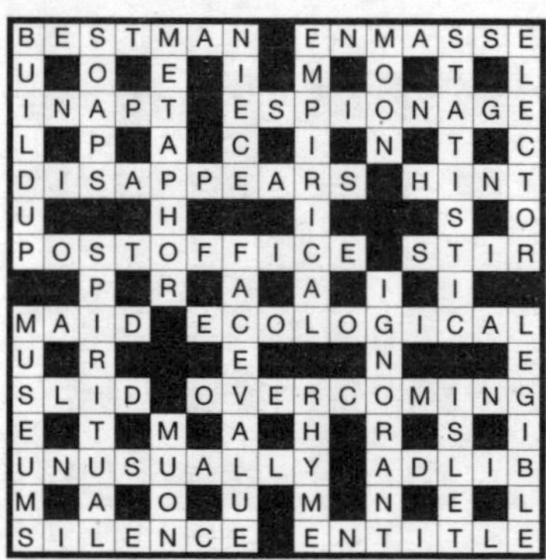

SOLUTIONS

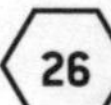

SOLUTIONS

28

SOLUTIONS

31

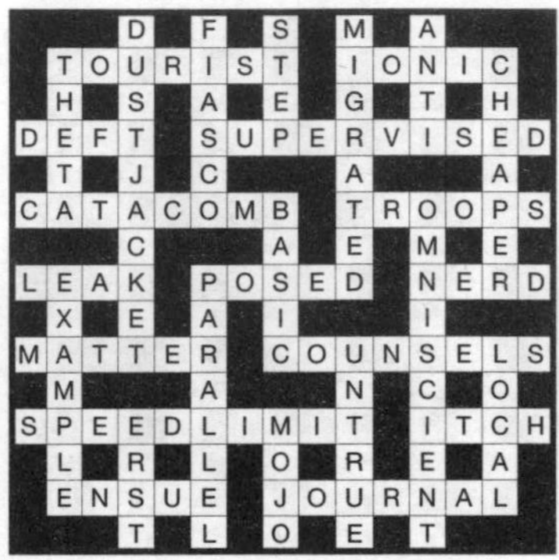

32

SOLUTIONS

33

DREAMED PERHAPS
E A E O A E L U
CITED OUTWEIGHS
O U I M R L O P
DEPRESSION TRUE
E V L I N
DRUGADDICT STUD
N L I A E H
HOPS ASTRONOMER
A O C V I
IMPS SUPPRESSES
R U D S O L E O
COLLAPSES OCTET
U A T E I P T T
THREATS TREMOLO

34

K S C M H F
SAUCE TINY OVAL
N R S R T R W
GARAGE COHERENT
P C L S O
RASP ROE CRIED
G E E S D L
CREDITS CASTOFF
E S A Y O I
PEKOE BET MINK
F E U I O
PREFIXES MARKED
U E I I E R D
HEAR SEND FOLIO
D S T G W T

SOLUTIONS

36

SOLUTIONS

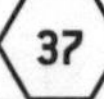

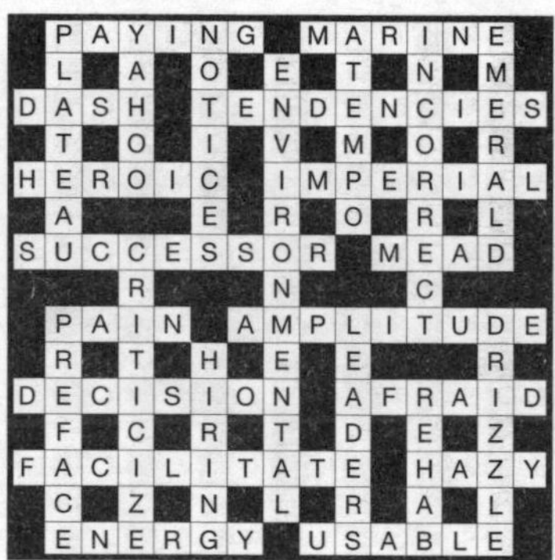

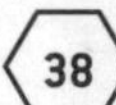

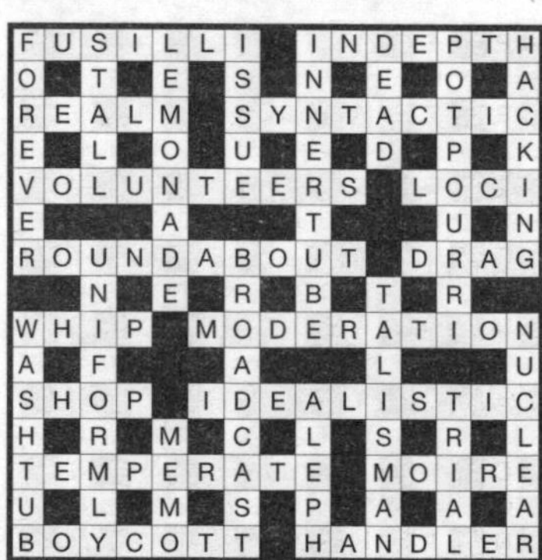

SOLUTIONS

39

40

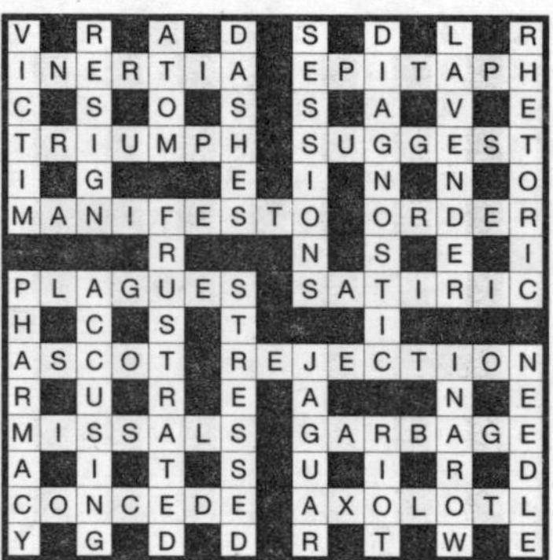

SOLUTIONS

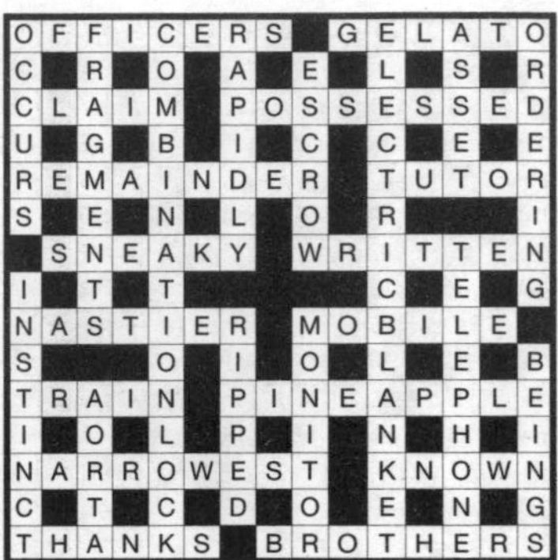

SOLUTIONS

SOLUTIONS

SOLUTIONS

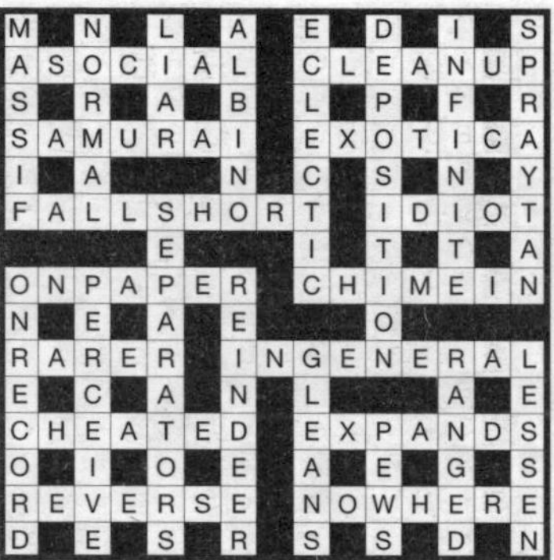

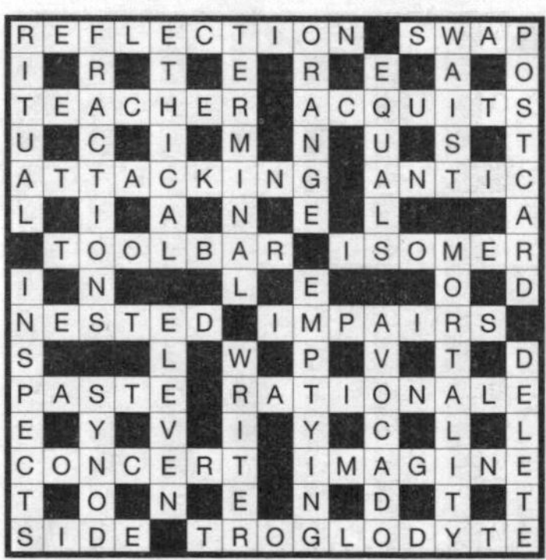

51

52

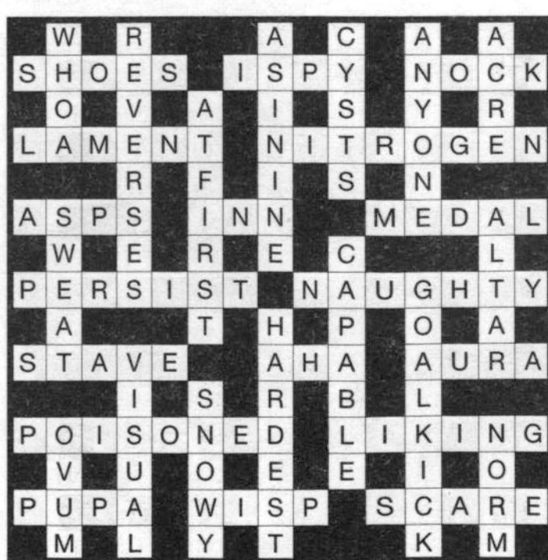

SOLUTIONS

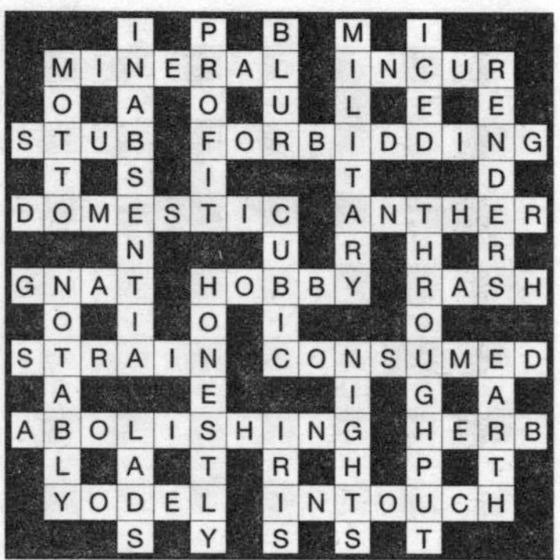

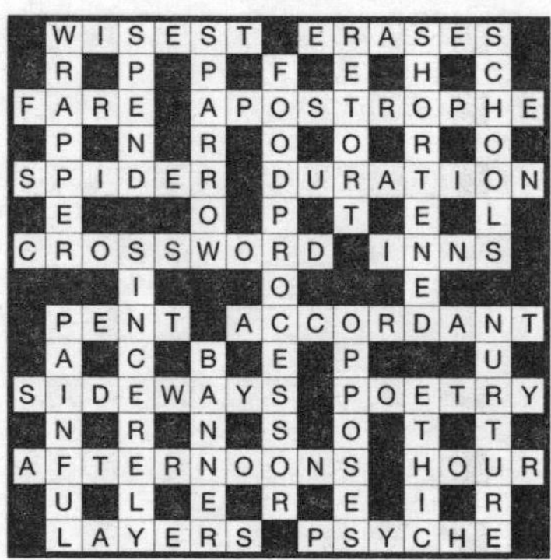

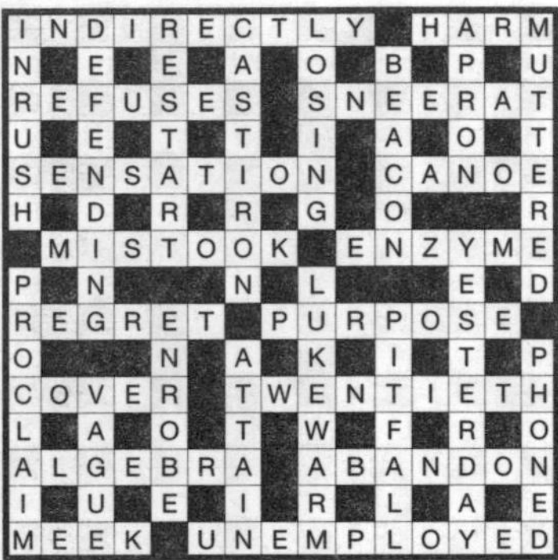

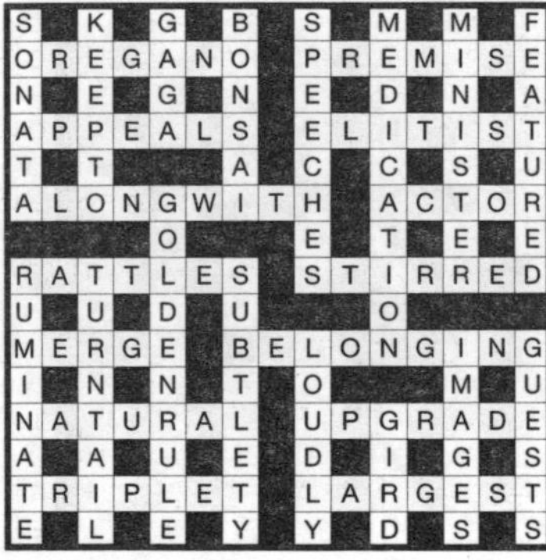

SOLUTIONS

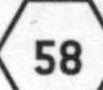

SOLUTIONS

SOLUTIONS

61

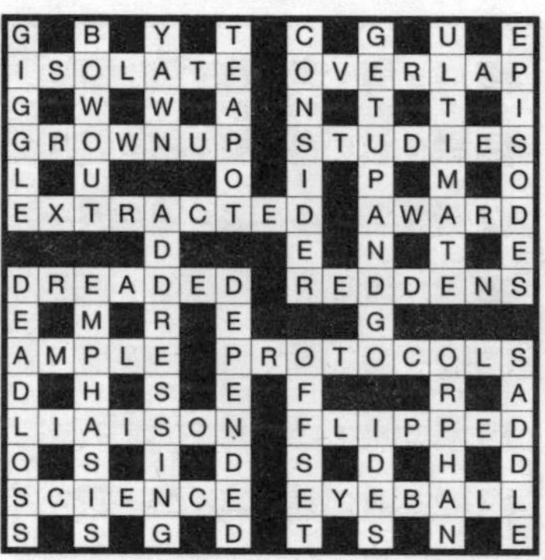

62

SOLUTIONS

63

COLLAPSING CALM
L A R U I J T O
IGNORES COUNTER
M D E T K N I E
BYMISTAKE GECKO
S A T I D L V
ARISING SEVERE
S K S S N R
KISSED JUSTIFY
E X O P E O A
LETGO PREFERRED
E H T T R N C A
TERMINI EXITING
O E C O G E N E
NOES ENCOURAGES

64

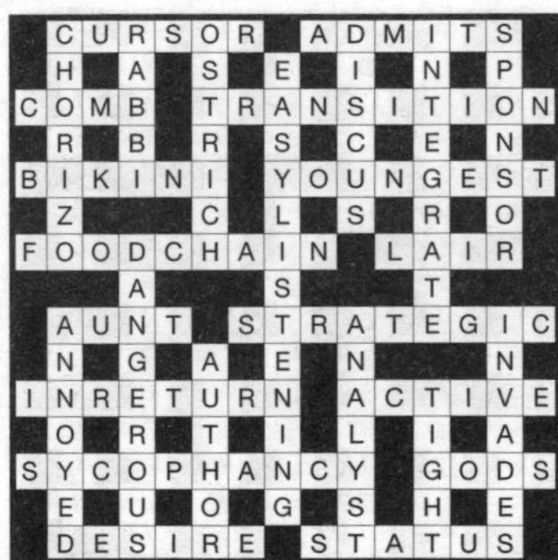
CURSOR ADMITS
H A S E I N P
COMB TRANSITION
R B R S C E N
BIKINI YOUNGEST
Z C L S R O
FOODCHAIN LAIR
A S T
AUNT STRATEGIC
N G A E N N
INRETURN ACTIVE
O R T I L I A
SYCOPHANCY GODS
E U O G S H E
DESIRE STATUS

65

FOCUSED TEDIOUS
A O E E O A R E
TULIP POLITICAL
I O A O E E H F
GENERATORS DELIS
U A A S S
EXCITEMENT ETCH
O E E C H R
IONS ACCELERATE
N T H A C
DUAL CANDIDATES
U I T N O A A T
CENTURIES COCOA
E E B S E H I S
SARCASM SWEETLY

66

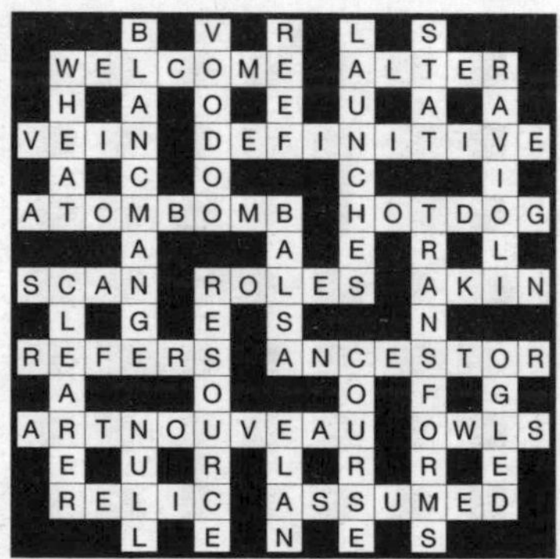

B V R L S
WELCOME ALTER
H A O E U A A
VEIN DEFINITIVE
A C O C I
ATOMBOMB HOTDOG
A A E R L
SCAN ROLES AKIN
L G E S N
REFERS ANCESTOR
A O O F G
ARTNOUVEAU OWLS
E U R L R R E
RELIC ASSUMED
L E N E S

SOLUTIONS

69

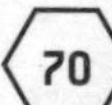
70

SOLUTIONS

71

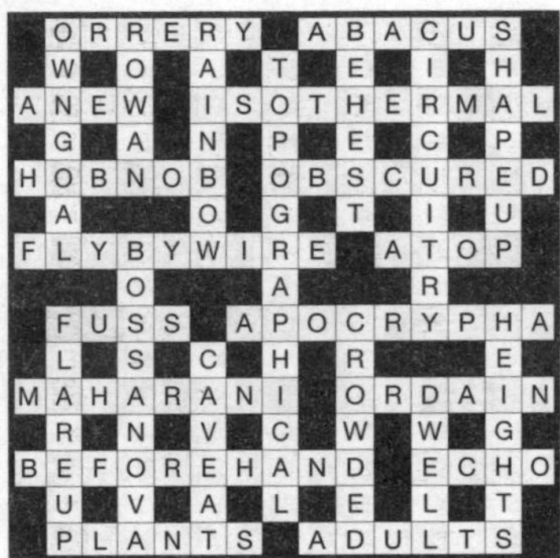

72

SOLUTIONS

73

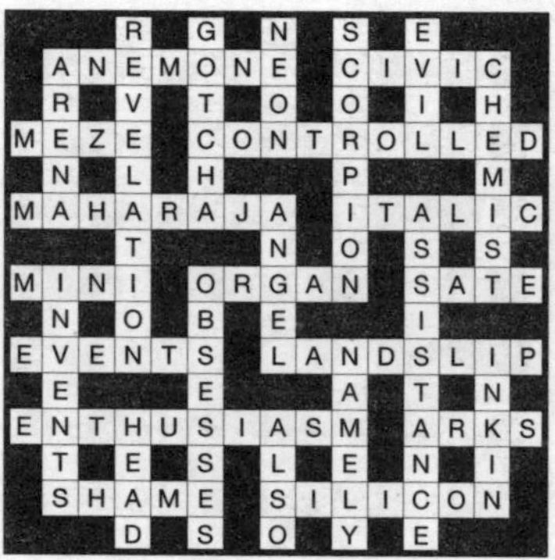

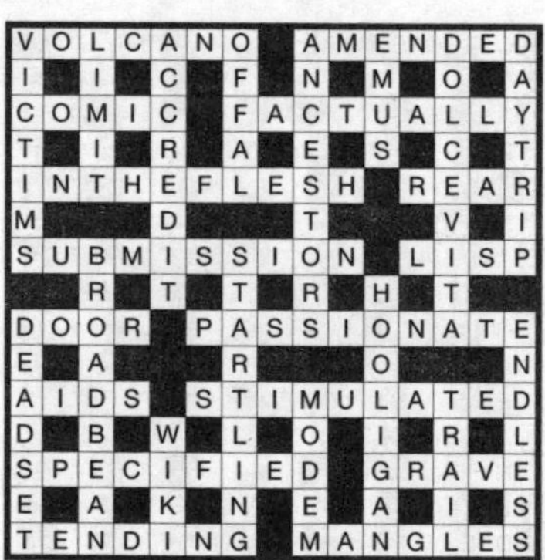

SOLUTIONS

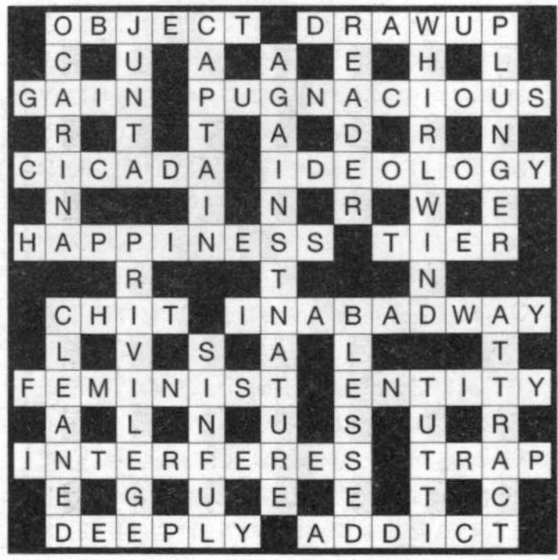

77

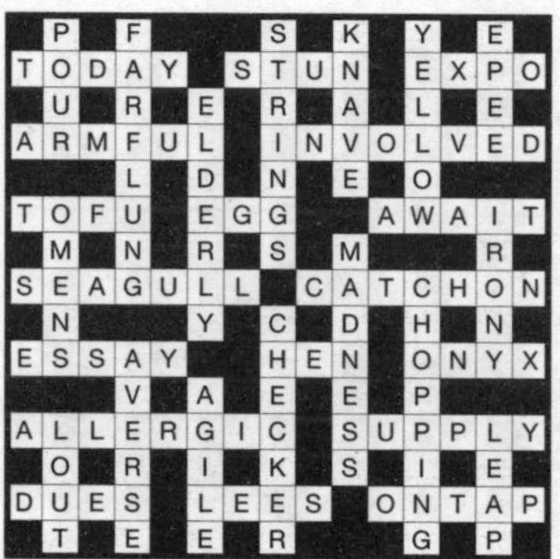

78

SOLUTIONS

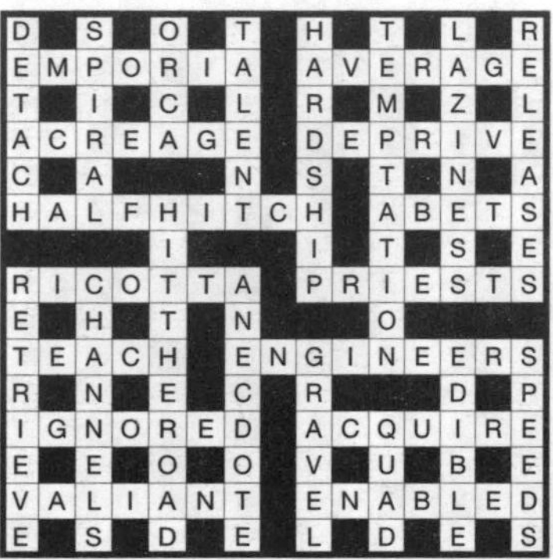

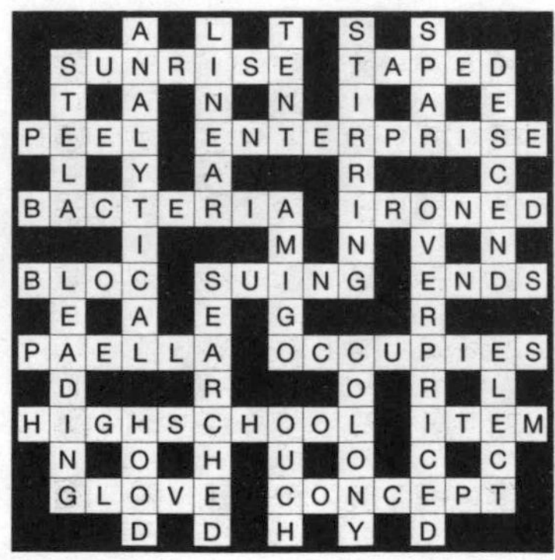

SOLUTIONS

81

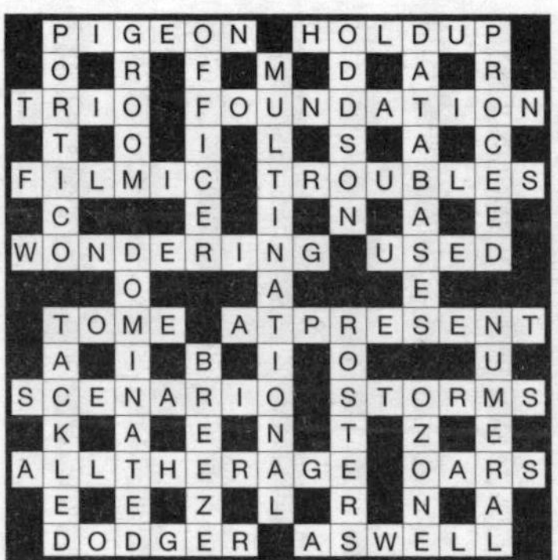
PIGEON HOLDUP
O R F M D A R
TRIO FOUNDATION
T O I L S A C
FILMIC TROUBLES
C E I N A E
WONDERING USED
O A E
TOME ATPRESENT
A I B I O U
SCENARIO STORMS
K A E N T Z E
ALLTHERAGE OARS
E E Z L R N A
DODGER ASWELL

82

E B I U C P
OVARY SNIP LOOP
E U A D S E L
ARENAS OPERATOR
E A U T N
KNIT RUB ASTER
O T U T W I
CUREALL PACKAGE
N E S S N H
USAGE HAS OATH
U S I A C
MAINTAIN IRKING
L G M I L I I
MOTH BONY INEPT
E O A G G S

SOLUTIONS

85

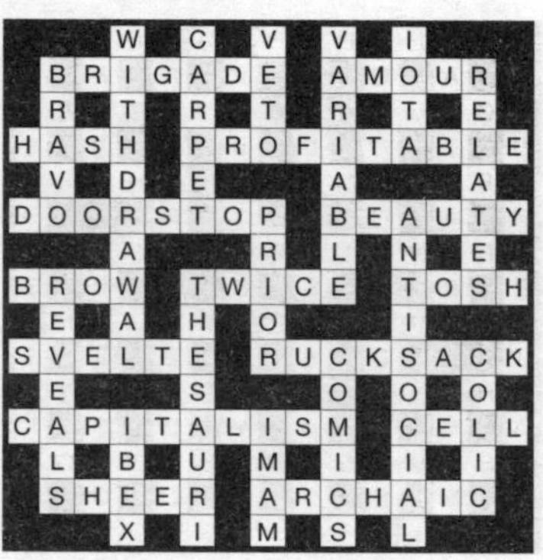

86

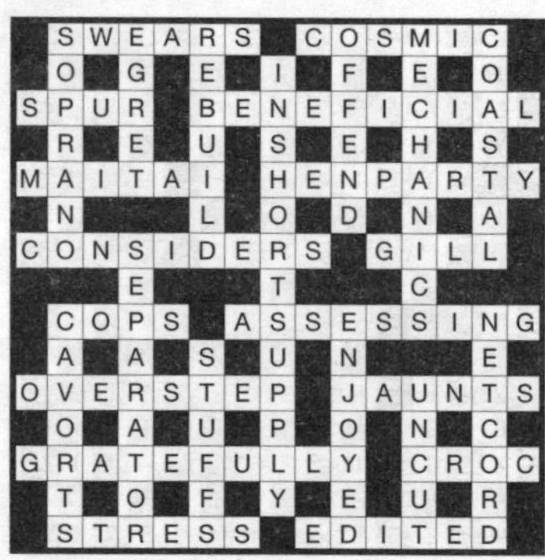

SOLUTIONS

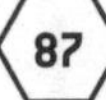
87

HUSHHUSH AFFAIR
E A O U P I P E
ACTUP FOOTNOTES
R I E F E I L P
TESTAMENT SAYSO
H F G R I H N
RIVALS CLIPPED
E E I N R S
PEDANTS REGION
I S A E S V T
THEFT DEFECTIVE
A N H D R H S N
PHENOMENA ONION
H M P N I O O I
STYLES INKLINGS

88

L A F S O A
VIEWS RAPT NONE
L A E S A L K
LYRICS TWILIGHT
T T E R N
MIDI ABS CELLS
D N T T A E
PLUGGED OPTIMAL
E S E P M V
USURP GAL MEET
E H O I A
MERCHANT EXTEND
X I I I D U I
TAMP ROSE CRACK
M E Y T E K

SOLUTIONS

89

90

SOLUTIONS

SOLUTIONS

SOLUTIONS

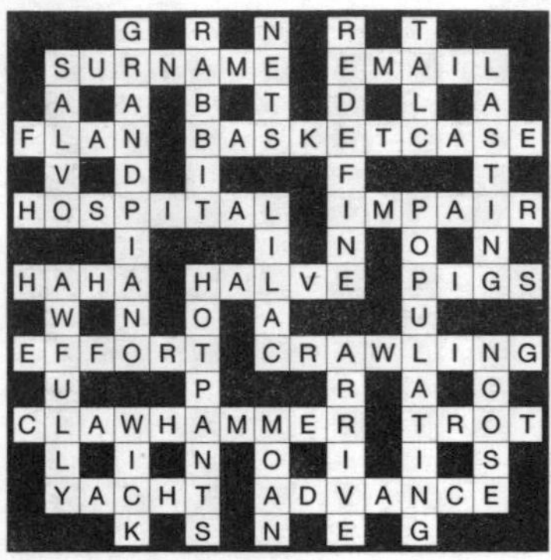

SOLUTIONS

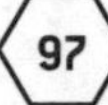

SOLUTIONS

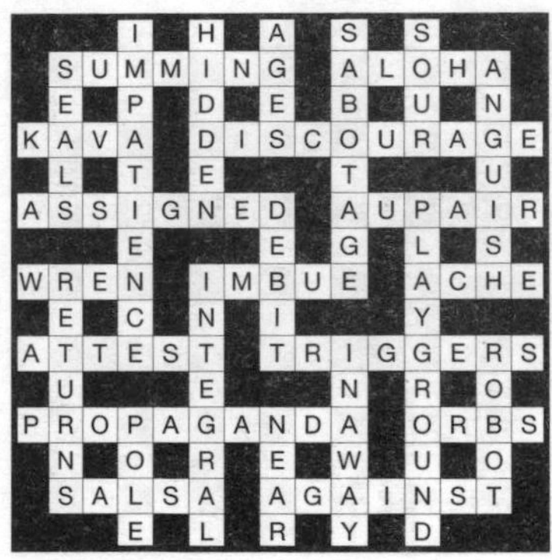

SOLUTIONS

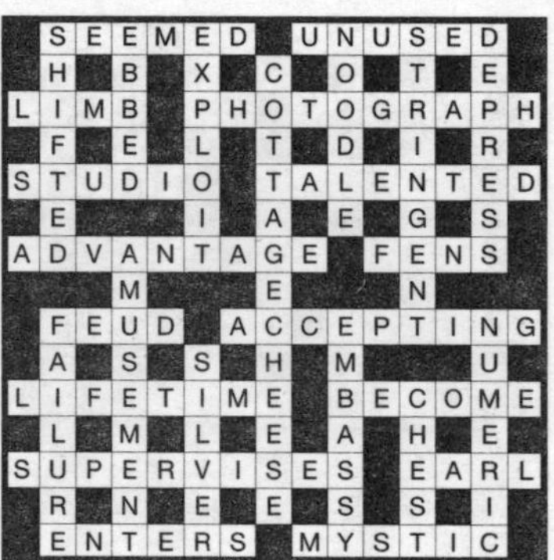

SOLUTIONS

103

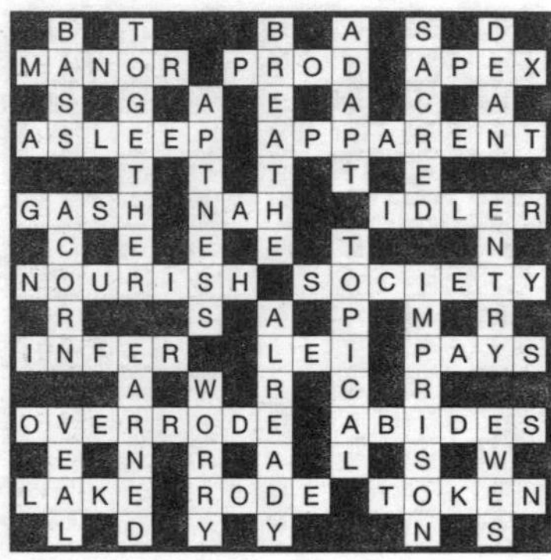

104

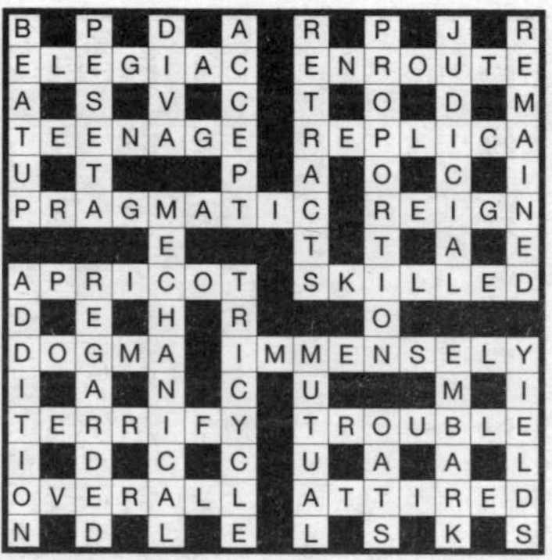

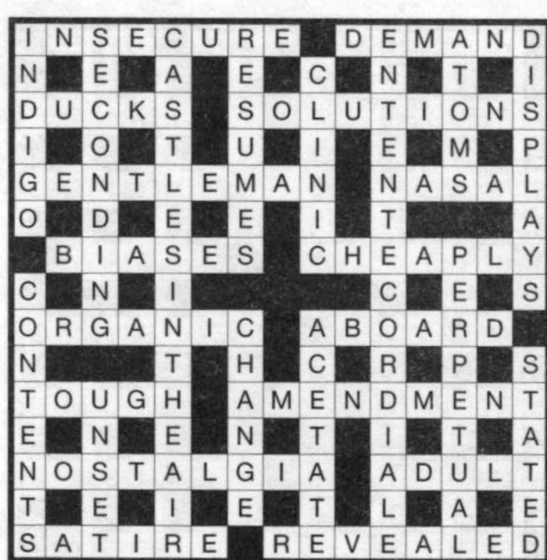

SOLUTIONS

107

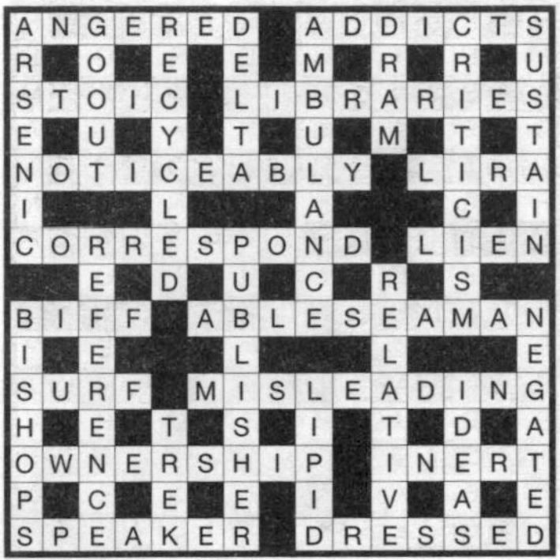

ANGERED ADDICTS
R O E E M R R U
STOIC LIBRARIES
E U Y T U M T T
NOTICEABLY LIRA
I L A C I
CORRESPOND LIEN
E D U C R S
BIFF ABLESEAMAN
I E L L E
SURF MISLEADING
H E T S I T D A
OWNERSHIP INERT
P C E E I V A E
SPEAKER DRESSED

108

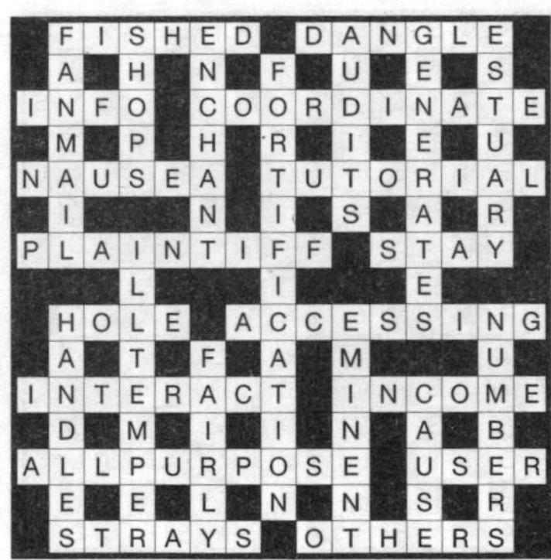

FISHED DANGLE
A H N F U E S
INFO COORDINATE
M P H R I E U
NAUSEA TUTORIAL
I N I S A R
PLAINTIFF STAY
L I E
HOLE ACCESSING
A T F A M U
INTERACT INCOME
D M I I N A B
ALLPURPOSE USER
E E L N N S R
STRAYS OTHERS

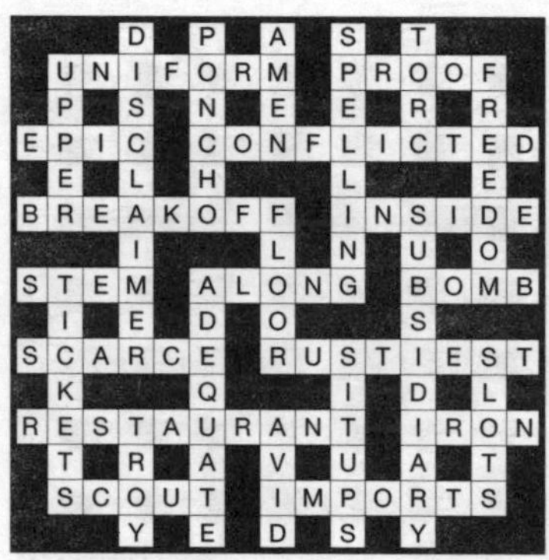

SOLUTIONS

SOLUTIONS

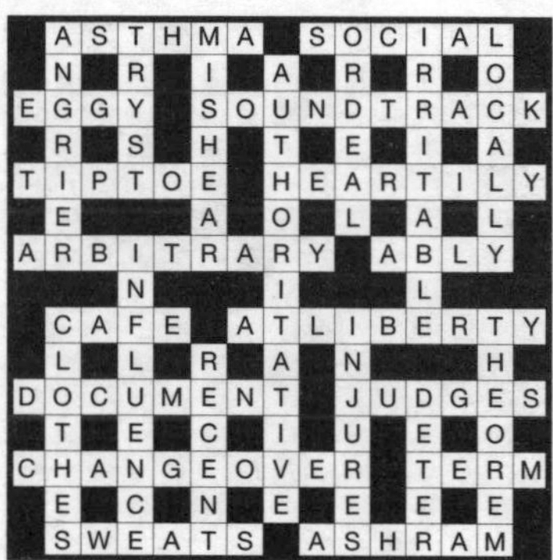

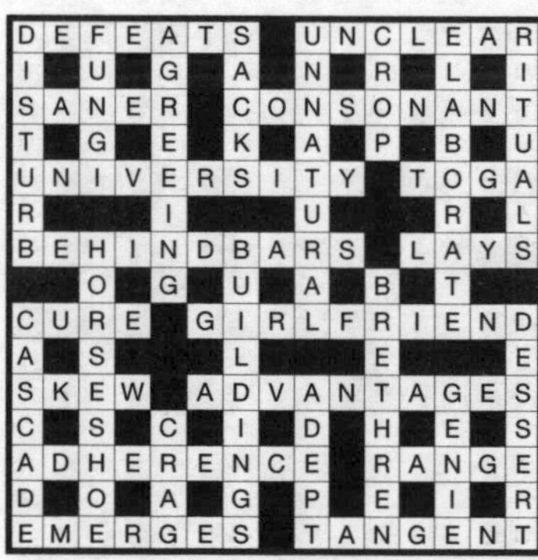

SOLUTIONS

117

118

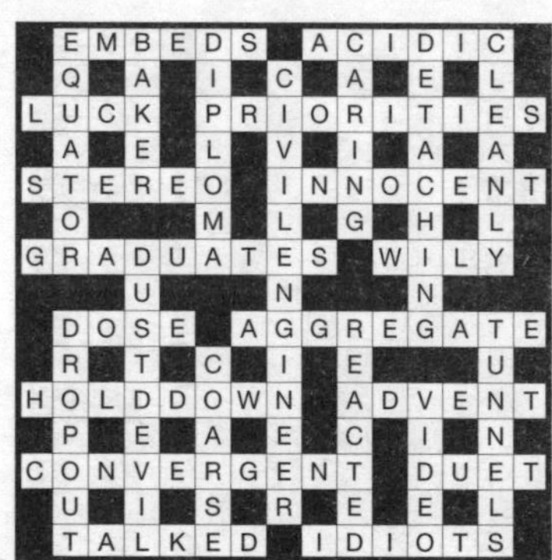

SOLUTIONS

NOTES

NOTES

NOTES